Praise for *Don't Jump to Solutions*

"Powerful, pragmatic, and jolting. A guide for how not to get trapped in one's own beliefs or those of the organization."
—JOHN SEELY BROWN, chief scientist and director, Xerox PARC

"Somehow Bill Rouse always seems to read my mind. His books give me a new perspective for my thinking on the very problems that are deviling our business right then. This latest treatise is no exception!"
—THOMAS R. OLIVER, chairman and CEO,
Holiday Inn Worldwide

"This is a powerful and practical handbook for organizational consultants as well as business leaders. For consultants, it provides data, examples, and tools to ask the right questions and to challenge the 'mental models' of business leaders. As many authors (Peter Senge, Chris Argyris, and others) have pointed out, mental models shape the way we act and many times become obstacles to successful implementation of strategy. *Don't Jump to Solutions* provides the means to test underlying beliefs and to begin to act strategically."
—JOYCE L. SHIELDS, PH.D., managing director,
Hay Management Consultants, Hay Group

"William Rouse has done an excellent job of identifying the key 'delusions' that often undermine strategic thinking. More importantly, he has developed a number of insightful strategies for moving beyond them. *Don't Jump to Solutions* is a thoughtful and helpful contribution to the current literature on strategic thinking and organizational planning."
—JOHN R. SEFFRIN, PH.D., CEO, American Cancer Society

"Any manager trying to invoke change in an organization should read this book. Knowing why we don't, helps [us] to do."
—THOMAS K. MANNING, CEO, The Rival Company

"Those submitting strategic planning and realization to the dictate of firmly established assumptions, structures, and behavioral patterns will find, while reading this book, the necessity and the courage to fundamentally reconsider these premises and to actively deal with alternative solutions."
—CHRISTOPH MEIER, managing director,
CIM Center for Western Switzerland (CCSO)

Also by William B. Rouse

Start Where You Are
Matching Your Strategy to Your Marketplace
ISBN 0-7879-0247-0

You can get there from here. Based on research and consulting involving more than one hundred companies, this strategically oriented book provides the tools and techniques you need to chart your company's future according to where it stands right now. The first book you should read before developing a strategic plan, *Start Where You Are* shows how to

- Assess where your organization stands in the marketplace
- Follow a step-by-step plan for determining your strategic situation
- Evaluate how your actions affect your organization's future
- Create your own business success story
- Take the first step in creating a strategic plan that will get your company where you want to be

"In a book laced with some captivating stories from the past, Bill Rouse's *Start Where You Are* elaborates on predictable patterns of business transitions. It provides some excellent lessons on embracing inevitable change and using it for strategic advantage along with some chilling reminders of the risk of past success and future business inertia."
—JIM PRENDERGAST, chief technologist
and director of strategy, Motorola

"Strategic plans are too often based on the erroneous assumption that the enterprise is in a relatively unchanging market environment where today's strategies will continue to work indefinitely. *Start Where You Are* provides an excellent set of concepts and tools to help you assess your current and potential future market situations so that the need for changing your strategies can be recognized before it is too late."
—DAVID W. GIVENS, director of strategic planning and business
development, Honeywell Space and Aviation Control

Available from Jossey-Bass Publishers
350 Sansome Street
San Francisco, CA 94104
(800)956-7739

Don't Jump to Solutions

Don't Jump to Solutions

Thirteen Delusions That Undermine Strategic Thinking

William B. Rouse

Jossey-Bass Publishers • San Francisco

Substantial discounts on bulk quantities of Jossey-Bass books are available to corporations, professional associations, and other organizations. For details and discount information, contact the special sales department at Jossey-Bass Inc., Publishers (415) 433-1740; Fax (800) 605-2665.

For sales outside the United States, please contact your local Simon & Schuster International Office.

Jossey-Bass Web address: http://www.josseybass.com

TCF Manufactured in the United States of America on Lyons Falls Turin Book. This paper is acid-free and 100 percent totally chlorine-free.

Library of Congress Cataloging-in-Publication Data

Rouse, William B.
    Don't jump to solutions: thirteen delusions that undermine strategic thinking / William B. Rouse.—1st ed.
        p. cm.—(The Jossey-Bass business & management series)
    Includes bibliographical references and index.
    ISBN 0–7879–0998–X (alk. paper)
    1. Strategic planning. I. Title. II. Series.
HD30.28.D6743   1998
658.4'012—dc21   97–33871

FIRST EDITION
HB Printing   10 9 8 7 6 5 4 3 2 1

The Jossey-Bass
Business & Management Series

Contents

Preface

Delusion:
 A persistent false belief not substantiated by sensory evidence

Strategic thinking involves asking yourself difficult questions. Finding the answers to the right questions can help you escape the tactical and operational concerns that often dominate the thinking of leaders in all types of organizations. To begin strategic planning, you should stand back, look at your organization, and ask

- What are the commonly held assumptions that underlie our vision?
- Have we challenged these assumptions?
- Will achieving our goals make a real difference in our future?
- Do our plans always lead to committed execution and to results?
- How important is it that our plans succeed exactly as expected?

Answering these and many other questions you will encounter in this book can help you identify and avoid delusions that can undermine strategic thinking. Delusions are not just bad assumptions. Delusions are persistent false beliefs that tend to become tightly woven into the culture of an organization. Often, data and facts will not dislodge these false beliefs. The only way to dispel them is to address them head on.

Consider the last strategic problem or decision your organization faced. Did you recognize potential delusions and, in light of the risks they posed, carefully assess the situation and formulate plans accordingly? Or were the pressures to "get on with it" such that you had to jump to a solution?

The questions I listed pertain to central issues in business strategy, marketing and sales plans, process reengineering, and so on.

To become really good at those things, you must learn to recognize typical organizational delusions; tough questioning will guide your effort to do that. If you are to excel, you must learn to avoid jumping to solutions while working under delusions.

Purpose and Intended Audience

The purpose of this book is to bring into the stark light of day the delusions that so often undermine strategic thinking and thereby derail goal setting, planning, and execution. My objective is to help you recognize these delusions and move beyond them. Thirteen delusions are particularly troublesome for a wide range of organizations. The delusions fall into four classes:

- Assumptions that become persistent false beliefs, despite the fact that they are no longer warranted or perhaps were never warranted
- Unspoken goals that often underlie and undermine stated goals, deterring organizations from achievements that will really make a difference
- Perceptions that plans will smoothly and easily lead to committed execution and sustained action
- Expectations that plans will not require fundamental organizational changes and that plans will succeed exactly as intended

In this book I describe the thirteen delusions, recommend central principles for recognizing and moving beyond them, and provide key questions to guide your use of these principles. I have written for those who lead or participate in strategic goal setting and planning in industry, government, academia, and volunteer organizations. I've drawn vignettes from, and described my own experience with, all these organizations. If you are a leader in industry, for example, you will benefit from seeing how the delusions manifest themselves in government or in volunteer groups.

The material in this book can be particularly valuable if you use it as follows. First, review the questions at the end of each chapter before you begin any major strategic planning activity. Second, use the questions to guide your review of any resulting strategic plans; the questions can serve as an audit instrument. Even though it is best to recognize and deal with delusions before you begin planning, it is better to identify delusions while plans are being completed than later during implementation.

Background

I have spent the last decade working with hundreds of enterprises and thousands of executives and senior managers. Most of my work has focused on developing new business strategies, creating new product plans, and facilitating substantial organizational changes. Almost all of these enterprises had adopted some form of continuous quality improvement, embraced some version of process reengineering, and invested substantially in whatever the best-seller lists of the *New York Times* and *BusinessWeek* told them was the latest and greatest prescription for organizational renewal and growth.

With these commitments came good news and bad news. The good news was that many of the things being done were valuable in that they helped create more efficient and effective organizations. The bad news was that some very useful concepts, principles, methods, and tools were not panaceas. They were often important bullets in the management gun, but they were not silver bullets. No magic solution can be provided by one or two books, or one or more seminars, or a few high-powered consultants.

How do enterprises develop and implement excellent plans? What is their secret? First of all, they know they have absolutely no choice but to develop such plans. Their markets may be disappearing, technologies are inevitably changing, and they are awash in current or potential crises. They have to act, and they know it. Put simply, they push aside delusions and develop a clear understanding of the strategic situations they face.

But why do the leaders of these enterprises understand their situations, and the vast majority of leaders do not? It's because the successful organizations have well-honed decision-making and problem-solving skills. Other organizations—the vast majority—suffer from a variety of delusions and do not develop those skills.

Here are a few examples. I have served on a variety of advisory committees for government agencies involved in managing the development of complex systems such as space stations, air traffic control systems, and military aircraft. In most of these endeavors,

I quickly learned that advice was not valued if it slowed in any way the agency's expenditures of billions of dollars. The overriding goal was to get on with it, regardless of what "it" was. These agencies suffered from the delusion that they knew what they were doing—that all of their assumptions were valid. Unfortunately, they were not always right, and they were far from unique.

Several of my experiences have involved planning in large volunteer organizations that were having trouble formulating their goals. The leaders tended to support the personal agendas of staff and key volunteers, whether these agendas were consistent with the mission of the organization or not. Reaching and maintaining consensus was more important—or at least more immediately pressing—than ensuring that the organization's plans were consistent with its stated goals. The real (but unstated) goal was to reach consensus, not to gain consistency with the organization's mission. Fortunately, planning processes that expose this delusion usually enable moving beyond it.

Many of my experiences are in industry—in planning new products in an existing product line, developing new product or service lines in current markets, and pursuing entirely new markets. Quite often, such efforts are cast as important elements in making major changes in companies. However, preserving the status quo can quickly become the predominant goal. Even though the real problem involves succeeding with new offerings, possibly in new markets, the de facto problem becomes one of finding ways to ensure that the players involved get to keep doing what they valued doing in the past. Commitment to change in situations like this is a delusion because avoiding substantive change is the underlying agenda. Appropriate planning processes can easily reveal this inclination, but it takes discipline to move beyond it.

I have many stories like this. They involve government agencies, major corporations, universities, religious denominations, and neighborhood associations. Organizational delusions—and decision-making and problem-solving deficiencies—are not limited to situations involving government projects or corporate product planning. These delusions also affect how problems are solved in running professional societies, building new church buildings, and discouraging beavers from clear-cutting the back yards of the neighborhood association members who live on the lake.

Thus, the importance of understanding common delusions and then avoiding them applies not only to your job and profession but to many of your professional and personal activities. As a consequence, the principles and guidelines presented in this book will help you in many of your endeavors. They will help you recognize typical organizational delusions, understand their consequences for decision making and problem solving, and assess your risks of jumping to solutions.

My path to understanding the impact of certain delusions began with a focus on planning. In *Design for Success* (Rouse, 1991), I discuss methods and tools for product planning. Use of these methods and tools in a variety of organizations led me to focus on business issues, as well as the methods and tools to address these issues, in *Strategies for Innovation* (1992). Difficulties implementing both product and business plans led to developing the methods for understanding and changing organizational belief systems that I present in *Catalysts for Change* (1993). An overview of all these methods and tools appears in *Best Laid Plans* (1994).

My intense involvement with planning in many organizations led me to wonder why planning is so difficult and why the execution of plans so often fails to deliver the desired results. It became increasingly clear that the *inputs* to planning often undermine the value of the *outputs*—the plans. Organizations often fail to understand where they are in the marketplace, as well as where their market relationships are most likely headed. This recognition led me to develop the assessment methods and tools discussed in *Start Where You Are* (1996).

Business strategies and plans that are premised on market relationships that you no longer have—or perhaps never had—inherently result in disappointing plans. If erroneous assumptions about market relationships persist despite repeated evidence of their falseness, the result is an organizational delusion—presented in this book as Delusion Three. Recognizing this led me to identify the full set of delusions I describe.

In writing this book, I came to realize that the methods and tools discussed in my earlier books are useful only if organizational delusions do not undermine strategic thinking. If delusions are rampant, the inputs to these methods and tools are inherently flawed. The result is flawed goals, strategies, and plans. Many methods and tools

are available for planning business strategies, new products, organizational changes, and so forth. If you understand and use the
material in this book, you can use any of them more productively.
This book will help you recognize and move beyond delusions, regardless of the procedures you employ for planning.

Overview of Contents

The book is divided into several sections. The Introduction sets the
stage; the Conclusions section focuses on putting the lessons
learned in the book to work; Parts One through Four, in between,
discuss the thirteen delusions that often underlie poor decision
making and problem solving.

Introduction

The Introduction focuses on the perils of acting first and thinking later—jumping to solutions. I discuss why deficiencies in the
decision-making and problem-solving abilities of organizations
often reflect delusions concerning assumptions, goals, plans, and
expectations.

I illustrate these delusions with vignettes drawn from my experiences with a wide range of enterprises. I discuss the basis for
the delusions in the context of principles from management and
psychology. I show why jumping to solutions is a natural and useful tendency most of the time—but a tendency that can sometimes
lead to regrettable actions.

Parts One through Four present four overarching rules for
avoiding the thirteen delusions:

- Challenge commonly held assumptions.
- Establish goals that make a difference.
- Make sure that plans lead to actions.
- Expect the unexpected.

Discussions of these rules lead, in each chapter, to Central Principles and to Key Questions you can use to help you avoid the delusions that undermine strategic thinking and decision making.

Part One: Challenge Commonly Held Assumptions

In this part, I discuss three assumptions that can be critical delusions. Delusion One: We Have a Great Plan deals with the inclination to mistake visions and plans for reality. This leads to past, often obsolete visions controlling how organizations address current problems. In contrast, visions should be dynamic; they should evolve as you learn from the unfolding reality of your organization and environment.

Delusion Two: We Are Number One considers the strong tendency for organizations to attribute to themselves greater skills and abilities than they actually have. As a consequence, people create what I call the *world class myth,* which mainly serves to impede their chances of improving beyond mediocre to average. They need to learn how to admit and understand their weaknesses. The ability to do that can become one of their greatest strengths.

Delusion Three: We Own the Market focuses on successful organizations' propensity for assuming that they own the markets or constituencies they currently serve. This assumption is frequently a precursor to losing track of their relationships with their markets and constituencies altogether, which typically leads to product or service failures that the organizations find difficult to explain. They need to learn to avoid attributing all successes to their skills and all failures to their bad luck.

Part Two: Establish Goals That Make a Difference

This part deals with five types of goals that often lead to delusions that undermine good decision making and problem solving.

Delusion Four: We Have Already Changed discusses the tendency to announce change when, in fact, the unstated and unrecognized goal is to preserve the status quo to the maximum extent possible. The usual result is that substantial energy is devoted to trying to make sense of and preserve old paradigms in new contexts.

However, effective strategy is about change. Effective change demands altering how people think and act, which demands setting goals that overturn the status quo. What is needed, therefore, are explicit decisions regarding what elements of the status quo should be kept and what elements should be discarded.

Delusion Five: We Know the Right Way considers how obsessions with technical correctness affect organizations' decision making and problem solving. When one discipline dominates—say, finance, marketing, or engineering—an aura of objectivity often emerges that skews everything toward that discipline's worldview. As a result, purely financial goals, for example, might govern the activities of marketing and engineering. Multidisciplinary teams are useful for avoiding this type of myopic decision making and problem solving.

Delusion Six: We Just Need One Big Win focuses on the common tendency to expect—and unfortunately wait for—a big win or sale that will solve all problems. I call this the *purple rhino syndrome*. This species is extremely rare, but when you catch a purple rhino, you can feast for a long time. Similarly, if you could just make that one big sale, everything would be okay. I argue that it is more useful to create a portfolio of appropriately diverse opportunities. That way, success does not depend on the frequent occurrence of rare events.

Delusion Seven: We Have Consensus deals with the quest for consensus, that is, getting everybody to agree despite conflicting values, priorities, and interests. This quest can smother valuable new points of view and limit creative confrontation. It is further complicated by the fact that disputes in organizations typically have sources much deeper than the surface features of the disagreements. People's needs and beliefs affect what knowledge is gained, what facts are sought, and how both are interpreted. Understanding this deeper source of perceptions can enable more creative approaches to consensus.

Delusion Eight: We Have to Make the Numbers discusses the frequent focus on short-term financial metrics. Decision making and problem solving often suffer due to organizations' inabilities to sacrifice short-term returns for potential long-term gains. We have become addicted to making the numbers. A good way to counterbalance this tendency is to decide on an appropriate balance between planning for the short term and the long term in your organization.

Part Three: Make Sure That Plans Lead to Actions

In this part, I discuss difficulties associated with implementing decisions and problem solutions.

Delusion Nine: We Have the Ducks Lined Up focuses on the tangled webs of relationships, often among a wide range of stakeholders, that sometimes must be navigated to make decisions and solve problems successfully. Not understanding these relationships, or perhaps understanding but discounting them, tends to lead to poor decisions or solutions, or at least to poor execution. This difficulty is best dealt with by developing explicit knowledge of the concerns, values, and perceptions of the many stakeholders in your success. This knowledge can enable creatively aligning the ducks.

Delusion Ten: We Have the Necessary Processes discusses the tendency of enterprises, particularly large institutions, to get in their own way. Decision making and problem solving related to external markets or internal processes can involve fundamental change. As companies, for example, attempt to cross over to new markets, they are inclined to want to keep as many of the old organizational structures and processes as possible. This baggage can block their path to success.

Delusion Eleven: We Just Have to Execute is concerned with maintaining commitment and action. It is common for the ball to get dropped, often because of the demands of old and obsolete processes. The past is usually compelling because people at least think they understand what happened and why. It is important to make sure that the future is more compelling than the past.

Part Four: Expect the Unexpected

This part deals with the fundamental reality of the nature of changes typically associated with making major decisions or solving major external or internal problems.

Delusion Twelve: We Found It Was Easy focuses on the processes of managing change. People expect that things will get back to normal once, for example, a new product is launched in a new market, but that doesn't usually happen. Internal changes are often needed if external change is to succeed. Although people may expect a bit of fine tuning, they are more likely to face a wholesale overhaul.

Delusion Thirteen: We Succeeded as We Planned discusses the fact that successful plans often succeed in ways that were *not* planned. Consequently, people are often surprised by the serendipitous nature of their successes. They may wonder whether it is worthwhile to plan at all. It is. Good plans place you in the path of serendipity. Good plans help you avoid diversions and know when true serendipity is at hand.

Conclusions: Beyond Delusions

In the final section, Conclusions: Beyond Delusions, I show how to detect and circumvent the thirteen delusions that undermine strategic thinking and decision making. I discuss seventy key questions that will help you lead your own management team in confronting their delusions. If you are an external facilitator, you will also find these guidelines invaluable.

Acknowledgments

The hundreds of stories and vignettes in this book are drawn from my experiences in leading or consulting with a large number of enterprises in the private and public sectors, academia, R&D (research and development) enterprises, and volunteer organizations. I am truly fortunate to have had these experiences. I am indebted to the thousands of executives, senior managers, and team members who have greatly contributed to my education. This book is my report on these many lessons.

Atlanta, Georgia   WILLIAM B. ROUSE
October 1997

The Author

William B. Rouse is chief executive officer of Enterprise Support Systems—a creator and provider of computer-based planning and assessment systems and tools, as well as related training and consulting services. He has served in leadership roles on the faculties of the Georgia Institute of Technology and the University of Illinois at Urbana-Champaign. He has also served in visiting positions on the faculties of Delft University of Technology in The Netherlands and Tufts University. He received his B.S. from the University of Rhode Island and his S.M. and Ph.D. from the Massachusetts Institute of Technology.

The author has thirty years of experience in engineering, management, and marketing related to information systems, decision support systems, and advanced training technology. His work has focused on complex organizational, process, and vehicle systems. In these areas, he has consulted with over one hundred enterprises in the private and public sectors, where he has worked with several thousand executives and senior managers. His expertise in these areas includes individual and organizational decision making and problem solving, as well as human-computer interaction and information system design. He has written hundreds of technical articles and reports and has authored many books, including most recently, *Start Where You Are* (Jossey-Bass, 1996), *Best Laid Plans* (Prentice Hall, 1994), *Catalysts for Change* (Wiley, 1993), *Strategies for Innovation* (Wiley, 1992), and *Design for Success* (Wiley, 1991). He edited the eight-volume series *Human/Technology Interaction in Complex Systems* (JAI Press) and has been featured in magazines such as *The Futurist, Competitive Edge,* and *Design News.*

Rouse is a member of the National Academy of Engineering, a fellow of the Institute of Electrical and Electronics Engineers (IEEE), and a fellow of the Human Factors and Ergonomics Society.

He received the Norbert Wiener Award from the IEEE Systems, Man, and Cybernetics Society, a Centennial Medal from IEEE, as well as the O. Hugo Schuck Award from the American Automation Control Council. He is listed in *Who's Who in America, Who's Who in Engineering,* and other biographical literature.

Introduction:
The Perils of Acting First
and Thinking Later

Have you ever decided to invest resources in solving a problem and later discovered that you were trying to solve the wrong problem? Have you ever found that your investment decision had little or no impact on your real problem? Many companies have had this experience.

General Motors invested billions of dollars in automation technology in the 1980s, only to discover much later that technology was not their problem (Taylor, 1992). Rather, they were producing increasingly out-of-date products. Automation did enable GM to produce higher-quality, lower-cost products, but it didn't help them produce the right products for the market.

Why does this happen? How are such poor decisions made? When pressed, decision makers usually say that, at the time, they did not understand the true problem they faced. They often say they did not have enough information.

Then why did they proceed? Many people say they *thought* they understood the situation and had the necessary information. The most common answer, however, is that they simply had to get on with it—that you can only collect information and analyze it for so long. At some point, you have to act.

They had to get on with it. They had to act. A bias for action is the hallmark of American business and society. Most of the time, this natural inclination is a key ability, but sometimes it can severely limit a company's potential for success. This poses a fundamental management problem: How can you overcome this limitation without undermining a key ability?

My goal in this book is to show you how to do it—to help you look before you leap but not ignore the caution that he who hesitates is lost. Although these two adages seem contradictory, they seem so only when you think you must choose between one of the two extremes. You don't. You can strike an appropriate balance between the extremes. In fact, you can gain substantial organizational leverage by doing just that.

A Few Examples

A key to achieving balance is to understand the natural human tendencies that, on occasion, need to be overcome if you are to avoid attempting to solve the wrong problems and thereby making the wrong decisions. Understanding natural tendencies can provide the basis for recognizing and avoiding jumping to solutions that are likely to lead to substantial regret. A few examples will illustrate some of these interrelated tendencies to act first and think later.

Investing in Noncompetitive Product Attributes

When approaching new product planning, companies often assume that they should play their strong suit. For example, technology companies' strong suit is often performance, such as their ability to create microprocessors that can process large amounts of information quickly, perhaps more quickly than any of their competitors' products can. Such companies tend to approach any competitive challenge by trying to improve the performance of their offerings. They assume that improving product performance is the way to go. The company culture fosters that pervasive and persistent belief, and it substantially affects their assumptions and their behavior.

The company invests money and people in an attempt to create a greater performance advantage. But it may be that cost, quality, size, power consumption, compatibility with other technologies, or other attributes are the key competitive issues. It may be that the marketplace cannot consume further performance improvements, perhaps due to other constraints. If that's the case, the market will perceive little if any benefit from improved performance. The company's investments will have been wasted. Of particular importance, the investments will have been based on a delusion that the company was solving the market's most important problem when, in fact, it was completely off target. (I discuss a variety of examples of this problem in the chapter, Delusion Three.)

Why does this happen? One answer is that jumping to solutions is a natural tendency. If a company's persistent, false beliefs—their delusions—had in fact been right, they would have been able to jump quickly and accurately. Another compelling answer is that people jump to things they know how to do. In this case, focusing on improving performance was something the company knew how to do. If they had focused on cost, for instance, it might not have been clear what to do. For people with hammers, everything in the world looks like a nail.

Preserving the Status Quo

Computer manufacturers have come to recognize the fact that computer hardware is increasingly becoming a commodity. The intensity of the competition among computer manufacturers has resulted in increased marketing and sales costs, but profit margins have eroded. Clearly, the halcyon days of manufacturing and selling computer hardware are over.

This recognition has prompted an important insight. Computer software companies are still able to achieve—and often exceed—the profit margins once enjoyed by the hardware manufacturers. Whereas hardware companies once gave away software to sell hardware, they now wonder whether they might be better off giving away hardware to sell software. They clearly see that software profits can replace their rapidly declining hardware profits.

Despite this understanding, strategic planning in these companies is dominated by a hardware perspective. Gut reactions and strategic decisions almost always emphasize bending metal (hardware) rather than bending bits (software). Even though they should be focused on transforming their company in the direction of software, they instead focus on preserving the status quo. (In the chapter Delusion Four, I discuss numerous examples of this tendency: the delusion of having changed.)

Consequently, companies such as Apple and Digital invest their resources in trying to become better hardware companies, when the real problem that needs investment is how to become providers of software. They may agree that they eventually need to move toward software, but today's resources get allocated to the status quo. The immediate benefit is that they get to do what they know how to do. It's probably the wrong thing to do. But, at least they know how to do it.

Trying to Get Around the System

The business world is not the exclusive province of these tendencies. The government is a rich source of illustrations. My next example is drawn from companies that do business with the U.S. Department of Defense (DOD), which has strict policies and procedures for, among other things, procurement and cost accounting. In one instance, these policies and procedures resulted in such delays that soon-to-be-obsolete computers were purchased, only to be replaced with computers that were also soon-to-be-obsolete, once they made it through the labyrinthine procurement process. As a result, substantial investments in converting software were necessary—twice.

At the same time, the contractor experienced large cost overruns in other areas of business with the DOD. Federal accounting regulations require that overruns be spread across all government contracts; the result was an almost 50 percent reduction of the person-hours devoted to this project. This reduction, combined with the fact that most of the person-hours had to be devoted to converting software twice, resulted in a dramatic reduction of the hours devoted to the effort for which the contractors were originally hired.

This vignette provides an excellent example of institutionalized conflicts that undermine everyone's best intentions. The result is that people focus on the wrong problem (for example, coping with the procurement system), in part because they have no choice. But at the same time, they share a delusion that the real problem is being solved. From the institution's point of view—in the example, the government's—the prevention of abuses is the goal of the system. In the process, however, the government sometimes prevents contractors from delivering solutions to the right problems. (As I illustrate in the chapter Delusion Ten, the government is not the only type of enterprise with such delusions.)

Modifying Appearances Rather Than Substance

Another example involves managing fundamental change. Many academic institutions are grappling with substantial changes in science, technology, education, and the outside world. They all want to think strategically and respond creatively to these forces. However, despite many meetings and much discussion, the result is the same in all cases. Real changes are minor. For the most part, departments and faculty keep doing what they have been doing. They do, however, re-label programs and activities to better match the current phraseology of research funding agencies and corporate constituencies. The delusion is that these new labels reflect fundamental change. However, without re-thinking their existing disciplinary paradigms and individually oriented reward structures, these adjustments constitute surface change at most.

The result of the delusion is a complete lack of response to external forces. Universities tend to manage change by modifying appearances rather than substance, so many different stakeholders are frustrated. This is not necessarily due to a lack of good intentions. It stems from a failure to recognize and formulate the real problems. (I discuss a number of examples of this phenomenon in the chapter Delusion Twelve.)

Summary

The four examples I have discussed in this section are just a few of the many stories and vignettes I use as illustrations throughout this book—illustrations drawn from the private and public sectors, as well as from academic, R&D, and volunteer organizations. No type of enterprise is immune from the delusions that underlie the tendency to jump to solutions. No organization can avoid the fact that this jump is sometimes ill-informed and premature. My goal is to help you know when to jump—and when not to.

Why People Jump

For many decades, researchers have been studying management problem solving and decision making. We now know quite a bit about people's abilities and natural inclinations in these areas—abilities and inclinations that are usually great strengths. Occasionally, however, strengths become weaknesses.

Natural Tendencies of Managers

Herbert Simon's Nobel-prize-winning studies of the behavior of managers provided the basis for many developments in economics, as well as in much of contemporary cognitive science. The results of his studies of the nature of management rationality are central to understanding people's inclination to jump to solutions.

In his book *Models of Man* (Simon, 1957), Simon introduces the concept of *satisficing*—a term meant to contrast with *optimizing*. Optimizers always make the best decision, carefully balancing all the relevant attributes of a situation. Satisficers make decisions that are "good enough." The likely consequences are satisfactory, even though they may be far from the best achievable.

Satisificing by managers greatly increases the acceptability of jumping to solutions. If all you need is a solution or decision that is good enough, then the chances of jumping inappropriately are substantially decreased. In this way, many decisions become much easier.

Another important body of work is that of Henry Mintzberg, who studied how managers spend their time. In a now-classic *Harvard Business Review* article, he debunks various myths about management (Mintzberg, 1975). Of particular importance to our discussions here, his studies reject the idea that managers are reflective, systematic planners. In contrast, managers are action-oriented and spend much of their time reacting to events around them. Their plans are far from elaborate and are usually in their heads.

Combine this perspective on management with the notion of satisficing, and it becomes clear why jumping to solutions is the norm. Managers typically have neither the time nor inclination to do otherwise. Further, making decisions that are *good enough* usually results in the company performing *pretty well*. Most will agree they could have done better, but the results are nevertheless satisfactory.

Jumping to solutions is not due to executives' and managers' limited abilities. Their problem-solving and decision-making behavior reflects the effects of typical company environments on managers, who must adapt to the ill-structured, ever-changing nature of both the marketplace and their own companies. Managers are inundated with issues, problems, and decisions, the vast majority of which are relatively minor. They satisfice and respond without reflection because it works. The time available for actions and reactions and the changing nature of decision situations tend to discourage reflective planning and trade-off studies.

The result is that delusions emerge and are unintentionally cultivated by organizations when there is little time for critical assessment. Assumptions are not articulated, and they are seldom challenged. Similarly, goals are quickly adopted and rarely questioned.

Difficulties That Promote Delusions

The emergence of delusions is not solely due to time pressures. Delusions are also fostered by most organizations' difficulties with strategic planning. Reflective, strategic thinking is a difficult task.

Recognition of the need to think strategically is an important first step—but it is only the first step. Several pitfalls must be avoided as thinking proceeds. All of these pitfalls are due to the natural inclinations of problem solvers and decision makers.

In *Best Laid Plans* (Rouse, 1994), I identify three common difficulties that people encounter when attempting to plan strategically. First, they are not sure what to do. They may use the word *strategic* in their discussions, but they tend to think tactically and operationally in the context they are familiar with (Hamel, 1996).

Second, whatever people choose to do relative to strategic planning, they take a very long time to do it. Often, there are endless time-consuming meetings and untold numbers of drafts of analyses and plans. This creates strong conflicts with the typical American business culture—with its bias for action and its desire for near-term rewards.

Third, and most problematic, when people are finished with planning, they often have not created anything they value. They submit, shelve, or file the plan, relieved that the process is finally over, and go about their business in the same way they would have if they had not created a plan. To a great extent, this is due to their having constrained planning to a familiar context (Hamel, 1996).

Thus, to simplify strategic planning, many organizations impose numerous constraints, many of which come in the form of persistent false beliefs—in other words, delusions. These constraints reflect managers' mental models of their organizations, markets, and so on (Senge, 1990). More specifically, managers are trapped by their belief systems concerning customers, performance, cost, service, and, in particular, the nature of innovation in their markets (Rouse, 1993). These false beliefs become delusions when they persist despite data indicating their falseness.

In their book *Blueprints for Innovation* (1996), Charles Prather and Lisa Gundry discuss several barriers to innovation, one of which is obeying nonexistent rules. The delusion is that the rules exist. This happens when rules that no longer exist are nevertheless still embedded in managers' mental models, which were formed from earlier experiences. This tendency underlies several of the delusions I discuss.

The consequence of these delusions, as Roger Martin (1993) points out, is that managers adopt old mechanisms for solving new problems and addressing new decisions. This is especially problematic for large organizations because these old mechanisms once suggested the right things to do. The delusion is that they still do. These managers' decisions and plans would be good if their old realities were still in place.

Making Delusions Visible

The obvious question concerns how to get managers' mental models aligned with new realities, that is, how to make delusions visible. To do this, people have to move beyond their typical internal focus and see themselves and their markets from an external point of view. In other words, managers need *outsight,* "the power of perceiving external realities" (Kouzes and Posner, 1987, p. 59).

In my book *Start Where You Are* (Rouse, 1996), I discuss the experiences of well over one hundred companies in the transportation, computer, and defense industries. I focus on the rise and, in most cases, fall of these companies and ask the simple question, Why? These case studies provide a clear answer. Most of the companies lost track of their relationships with their markets. They became very insular, assuming that the relationships that had led to their success would continue. This persistent belief became a delusion—one that proved to be their undoing.

How can companies make their delusions visible? Dorothy Leonard-Barton, in *Wellsprings of Knowledge* (1995), suggests anthropological expeditions to discover the external world. In *Best Laid Plans* (Rouse, 1994), I advocate a similar construct—the naturalist phase—as a precursor to strategic planning. The naturalist phase focuses on exploring and gaining an organic understanding of the natural environment that you hope to affect. The primary skills needed are observing and, especially, listening. The Central Principles and Key Questions at the end of each chapter in this book provide guidance on issues to consider when "naturalizing."

It is important to note that delusions are not only unearthed during strategic planning. As James Collins and Jerry Porras point out in *Built to Last* (1994), "In examining the history of the visionary companies, we were struck by how often they made some of their best moves not by detailed strategic planning, but rather by experimentation, trial and error, opportunism, and—quite literally—accident" (p. 141). Challenging assumptions is key to the experimentation and opportunism that are paying off handsomely for Hewlett-Packard, Motorola, 3M, and others. These companies know how to chose goals that will make a difference and to ensure that plans lead to actions.

Central Themes

Persistent false beliefs—delusions—emerge naturally in all organizations. My goal in this book is to help you understand delusions, recognize them when they emerge, and know how to circumvent them. A few highly interrelated themes form the book's core.

First and foremost, I hope to convince you that despite the merits of a bias for action, Tom Peters's exhortation, "Ready, fire, aim" is unsound advice (Peters and Waterman, 1982). Certainly, the paralysis of analysis should be avoided, but the other extreme provides an equally poor basis for running your organization.

Second, wanting to get on with it is natural. This strong inclination often preempts understanding what "it" really is. However, the simple fact is that throwing resources—people, money, and time—at problems seldom works. If it did, NASA would have had a space station long ago, General Motors would still dominate the automobile industry, and International Business Machines would still rule the world of computers. These are but a few of many examples of resource-rich enterprises investing in the wrong things.

A third theme concerns people's proclivities to invest in the wrong things because they do not understand the underlying nature of the situations in which they find themselves. One or more delusions preclude them from understanding their true problems. Unchallenged assumptions and unspoken goals predominate, and the natural tendency to jump to solutions prevails.

For most of life's activities, this reaction is both efficient and effective. However, when substantial resources and consequences are involved, it pays to question assumptions and goals, understand likely execution difficulties, and create mechanisms for monitoring results. In such situations, the tendency to jump to solutions usually results in an efficient path to an ineffective solution.

Because a bias for action, avoidance of planning, and lack of questioning of key assumptions are natural, often useful, human tendencies, the question is not how to eliminate them. The issue is how to overcome them when they are inappropriate, that is, when they are based on delusions that will undermine strategic thinking and decision making. We must recognize when to refrain from acting immediately; we must learn when to pause and explore potential delusions. That is the only way to ensure that delusions are not leading us astray.

Part One

Challenge Commonly Held Assumptions

We Have a Great Plan
Comparing Visions and Realities

Do you have a strategic plan that describes your business intentions with regard to market opportunities, major competitors, products, services, technologies, sales channels, and so on? When did you last review the assumptions underlying your plan? How certain are you that these assumptions are still reasonable?

This chapter, as well as the following two chapters, will show you how to challenge commonly held assumptions. Thinking that begins with bad assumptions usually results in bad plans—bad in the sense that they cannot possibly lead to achieving the goals that prompted you to plan in the first place. Many companies, as well as other types of enterprises, begin planning with the following unstated, and hence unquestioned, assumptions:

- Steady and substantial progress is being made toward our shared vision and goals.
- Our organization excels at all the competencies necessary for achieving our goals and realizing our vision.
- The marketplace is predisposed to accepting and buying our offerings rather than considering those of our competitors.

These assumptions usually need to be challenged. This chapter focuses on the first assumption; the next two chapters address the other two.

Visions, Missions, and Goals

The importance of having a corporate vision is often emphasized. A vision is an image of success that portrays where the organization is going and what it will look like, both along the way to success and when success is achieved. A mission, in contrast, is a statement of an organization's values. A mission statement answers these basic questions: Who are the customers or constituents? Where are they located? What benefits does the organization provide them? and How are those benefits provided?

Visions tend to motivate the people who work in an organization, whereas missions tend to compel people to buy products and services from the organization. Relationships between visions and missions are of particular interest in this chapter.

Most organizations have either explicit or implicit visions. In many organizations, visions are translated into a series of goals or accomplishments to pursue. Strategies are then developed for achieving these goals. Progress in executing the strategies provides evidence of progress in realizing the visions.

For example, a common vision is that of transforming a new technology into a product or service that can provide a substantial competitive advantage in the marketplace. Pursuit of this vision is likely to involve goals such as completing initial market studies, developing a first version of a product, evaluating a prototype manufacturing process, and so on. I have seen countless plans with this type of vision and these kinds of goals.

Visions like this are compelling. It is easy to sense the excitement and commitment of the people involved. Everyone is intent on doing great things. Many are also aware of the rewards that will come with succeeding. However, the vision of the tangible product or service is usually the most compelling element of this picture.

This is the way great plans and expectations are launched. Then reality intervenes, and various things start to happen: the results of the initial market study are ambiguous; the initial version of the product consumes too much power; the yields from the prototype manufacturing process are much too low; competitors make announcements; new technologies appear on the horizon.

Six to twelve months later, the plan gets revisited. Everyone is aware that things are not going as smoothly as expected. Attention is invariably focused on fixing the plan. What changes are needed in marketing, engineering, and manufacturing? How will these changes affect the schedule and budget?

Rarely do people sit back and examine their vision in light of the aforementioned events. This is easy to understand. They are already completely sold; their egos are invested in the vision. Rather than question their premises, they are drawn to fixing the problems that seem to be hindering their progress toward realizing the vision.

A primary difficulty with questioning the vision is imagining what you will do if you find it to be fundamentally flawed. But this difficulty can be avoided. Rather than consider rejecting the current vision, you should put it aside temporarily, then ask yourself: Given the experiences of the past six to twelve months, what vision will work with our company's markets and technologies?

This question often produces more than one answer, especially if you really *have* put the current vision aside. You then compare each of these alternatives to your current vision. For this comparison you ask, How might our current vision be changed to take advantage of elements of the alternative vision?

This question should produce a list of possible changes, which are seldom compatible. This leads to an in-depth discussion of the benefits and costs of each change. It almost always leads to one or more changes being adopted. Having made these selections, you then revise your plans.

Comparing Visions and Realities

The overall issue has to do with what you've been trying to make happen as opposed to what seems to *be* happening. In other words, the issue is visions versus realities. Several examples will show the underlying nature of this problem and how to deal with it.

Initial Visions

I have worked with quite a few start-up companies, many of which have been university spin-offs. Several of these I helped found. Other companies were clients for my company's planning tools and services. Even though the examples are different, the stories are similar.

Russ Hunt and I founded a company called Search Technology. We had a vision of commercializing the technologies for training simulators and decision support systems that we had developed at the University of Illinois. Another example is a firm that spun off from MIT, whose owners had a vision of applying control technologies to military command and control. Another is a company formed by Georgia Tech faculty members who had a vision of developing computer software and related services for the design and operation of distribution networks. Yet another is a company that spun off from MIT; the owners had a vision of commercializing high-efficiency energy storage systems.

All of these companies remain successful after having been in business, in some cases, for almost twenty years. They have all experienced periods of strong growth and occasional setbacks. None has experienced truly explosive growth. None dominates a market. The original vision has been only partially realized.

These are typical stories about slow, steady growth and moderate success. Apple, Microsoft, and Netscape are aberrations—statistical outliers. Success like theirs hardly ever happens. Yet, we've come to expect it; this is a common vision.

As a consequence, expectations are often unmet. A key question in planning, then, is whether or not the original vision is still realistic. Perhaps the market is not ready, and it will take much longer to realize the vision—perhaps many years longer. Another possibility is that new competitors and new technologies have all but eliminated the anticipated competitive advantage.

For example, at Search Technology we learned that our training technology was too expensive for all but relatively cost-insensitive customers such as the government and regulated industries. We also learned that the adoption process for decision support technology is quite slow in complex domains like aerospace and military systems. This resulted in our business being dominated by low-margin, contracted R&D efforts. Subsequently, we moved into the business systems market where adoption tends to be faster.

We eventually challenged the original vision. We should have done it earlier, but our reluctance is typical. Most start-up companies are driven by visions in which the owners have substantial ego investment. They have created technological children, and they are determined that these technologies will succeed in particular ways. However, as with human children, you sometimes have to question your assumptions and let them succeed in ways you had not imagined.

Evolving Visions

For all sizes of enterprises, technology development provides a rich context within which to view the ways visions can be either the sails that propel us forward or the anchors that hold us back. The process of developing new ways of doing things usually begins with a vision of how something new can be accomplished, or at least accomplished differently. This vision drives developers to invest themselves and their resources. However, this drive does not always lead to success. It especially does not lead to success in the ways developers anticipated.

A few examples will illustrate this point. In the early 1970s, we conducted a series of studies focused on why people such as air traffic controllers were often unable to predict the paths of the aircraft they were tracking. While this is a difficult task, it isn't impossible. We wondered why prediction was problematic. Studies of this and similar tasks led us to conclude that people have difficulty gaining and maintaining accurate mental models of the dynamic things they track, whether aircraft, ships, or the stock market. By mental models, I mean mental representations that enable people to form expectations about what will happen, as well as infer explanations of things that have happened.

The implication of this conclusion is that people should be given aids for performing such tasks. We pursued this possibility for a while but could not find an opportunity to use what we were learning. We published a summary article on these types of studies (our own and those of others) in the mid-1980s. This article led an organization to ask us about the possibility that members of skilled teams can have mental models of each other's roles—models that enable them to predict what each team member will do, as well as make sense of their observations of each other.

Studies of this possibility in the early 1990s led us to the conclusion that deficient mental models could explain poor team communication and coordination. We subsequently developed a computer-based training system to enhance people's mental models. Evaluations of this new type of training showed that it led to substantial improvements.

This example illustrates how a technology—in this case, a behavioral technology—emerged from R&D. Our initial vision of how the technology could benefit air traffic controllers and similar personnel did not bear fruit. Eventually, the technology did contribute to solving an important problem, though it was far removed from the one we had originally envisioned.

Another example relates to developing a new type of training simulator. This effort started in the late 1970s with a series of studies of library networks designed to enable library patrons to use the resources of the large number of libraries across the state of Illinois. We wanted to develop a method for determining the best path for requests to take through the network in light of the probabilities of success and potential delays at the many libraries (nodes) in the network. A potential path could be graphically portrayed as a path among the nodes in a network diagram.

It struck us that diagnosing the problems with particular paths was as important as being able to generate alternative paths. We soon realized that we were talking about troubleshooting in general rather than just routing requests for library materials. This led to a series of studies of people's abilities to troubleshoot, that is, diagnose problems, in network representations of several different kinds of problems.

The results of these studies indicated a variety of human limitations in this task. Of more practical importance, however, we found that use of our network simulations led people to become better and better troubleshooters. Our laboratory device was an excellent training simulator, although that was never our intention. We soon found funding to develop the technology further.

We evaluated the idea for applications in troubleshooting automobiles, aircraft, ships, communications systems, nuclear power plants, and spacecraft, which led to identifying the conditions under which training like this most enhanced human performance. By the late 1980s, personnel in a variety of industries were being trained using versions of this type of simulation technology.

This technology development effort began with funding from NASA. Subsequent customers included the U.S. Army, the commercial marine industry, the utility industry, and the U.S. Air Force. The idea succeeded because we persisted in finding customer after customer. We adapted the vision to the dynamics of the marketplace. We let the realities of customers' needs and priorities determine the ways in which the vision evolved. Had we stuck steadfastly to the original vision, the result at most would have been an interesting set of studies.

A third and final example relates to the way people interact with "intelligent" computers. This development effort began in the mid-1970s in the context of pilots interacting with artificially intelligent computers designed to help them fly their airplanes. Our initial efforts resulted in observations of what we termed *conflicting intelligence*—two intelligent entities (humans and computers) working at cross-purposes and, in this case, precipitating dire consequences.

This observation led us to develop analytical models of how two intelligent entities can cooperate. Experiments with these models showed us that cooperation depends on the computer "understanding" its users—the pilots and other crew members. We called this concept the *intelligent cockpit*. We also designed the specific functionality necessary for the computer to have this level of intelligence.

These efforts in the late 1970s and early 1980s got people's attention, which led to contracts in the last half of the 1980s and early 1990s to create practical demonstrations of the intelligent cockpit and to collect data to prove the value of this intelligent systems technology. In recent years, we have been working to further refine the technology and get it adopted for use in both commercial and military aircraft.

The path to adoption is complicated. For a commercial aircraft manufacturer to adopt a technology, it will have to be desired by at least one major airline; one or more avionics companies will have to be willing to include the technology in the systems they provide the aircraft manufacturer; and the Federal Aviation Administration will have to approve its use. And, of course, pilots, their unions, and aviation industry associations must be supportive. Lining up all these stakeholders is a time-consuming task.

Our current best estimate is that one of the basic elements of this technology will be flying in airplanes by the early 2000s. Assuming that this happens, the time from the initial vision to realization of a piece of the vision will have been roughly thirty years. Such lengths of time are often realistic for technology development.

The implication is that evolution rather than revolution is the usual rate of progress. When reviewing your vision and comparing it to reality, it is important to focus on your assumptions regarding the time frame in which the vision is likely to be realized. Put simply, your plan must include a means for keeping your bread buttered while you reach for the elusive brass ring.

Central Principles

The lessons learned in this chapter can be summarized in the vision principles listed in Exhibit 1.1. These principles provide a basis for avoiding the delusion that your original vision is on track—a delusion that can ruin your business.

The stories I have told are typical. Thousands of similar stories are associated with the development of various new ways of doing things. An excellent source of such stories is the fascinating quarterly magazine *Invention & Technology,* published by Forbes, Inc. While each story is unique, all of the stories provide similar lessons about vision quests.

First of all, innovation—getting the world to do things differently—almost always takes longer than anyone expects. A meaningful comparison of your vision and reality must take account of the pace at which innovation is taking place. Can you accept that pace of progress?

Second, the vision that launched you (or Ford or IBM) is just the starting point. Your vision needs to be dynamic and should change as the market and technologies change. In contrast, static visions always lead to eventual failure.

Third, if you are open to it, serendipity can substantially change your vision and lead to greater success. I don't mean that it will cause you to change from building airplanes to making donuts. However,

---

Exhibit 1.1. Vision Principles.

- On a regular basis, step back, examine your vision, and compare it to current realities; the sooner you can find substantial mismatches, the less likely you are to fail.

- Most change happens in an evolutionary rather than revolutionary manner; make sure the expected time frame in your plan reflects this reality.

- Your vision should be dynamic and evolve as you learn; use your ongoing experiences in markets, technologies, and so forth to continually refine and revise your vision.

- Your vision is unlikely to be realized in the ways you anticipate; be open to serendipitous ways to achieve success.

it certainly could mean that your technology provides its greatest competitive advantage in ways you might not have imagined.

Key Questions

The first element of challenging commonly held assumptions involves comparing your vision to reality. Exhibit 1.2 summarizes several key questions to ask when making this comparison. The questions embody the lessons just discussed.

The last question on this list is new. Once you have answered all the other questions in the list, this last question addresses the bottom-line issue: Is your original vision still compelling? Is the modified vision now compelling?

If your answer is no, you have some basic work to do. You need to focus on creating a compelling vision. The best place to start is with your current or potential customers. Use a cross-functional team of people from your company to interview—and listen to—your customers. These interviews should provide the raw material for creating a new vision.

If your answer is yes, we are ready to proceed to other types of assumptions that should be challenged. After challenging your vision, we need to challenge your ability to realize this vision. We then move on to challenge the success potential of this vision from the market's point of view.

Exhibit 1.2. Comparing Visions and Realities.

- In what specific ways do your vision and reality differ?
- How does the expected pace of realizing your vision compare to the actual pace?
- Does your plan need to be modified to reflect more realistic expectations?
- In light of current realities, what new visions are possible and likely?
- What elements of these new visions can be incorporated into your vision?
- Is your vision, perhaps as modified for current realities, still compelling?

We Are Number One
Letting Go of the World Class Myth

Does your management team include people in marketing, sales, engineering, manufacturing, finance, and perhaps human resources and information technology? How strong is this team? It is quite common to feel that every team member is first rate, or perhaps even world class. At the very least, people usually feel that all their team members are above average.

It seems that every organization I work with includes only people who are above average. Many executives and managers tell me that everyone in their organization is above average—far above average. Further, everyone has superior ideas, feels high levels of commitment, and produces superior results.

Two explanations are possible for this statistical aberration. I may simply be missing those organizations in which everyone is below average—where everything goes wrong, and where it always looks like the bull has just passed through the china shop.

The other explanation is that the people I talk with are wrong. Their assertions contribute to the perpetuation of a myth. It is impossible for everyone to be world class. Nevertheless, people and organizations tend to believe this myth, or at least act in accordance with it. As a consequence, they tend to ignore people's limitations and shortcomings.

Dogmatic adherence to the world class myth results in plans that are never completed, finished plans that are never implemented, and executed plans that do not meet expectations. The reason is that believers of the myth ignore, or at least do not address, the real problems underlying poor or mediocre performance.

This chapter concerns the impact of the world class myth on individual and organizational performance. What happens when individuals within an organization, and the organization as a whole, feel that they are as good as it gets? Further, what happens when everyone feels that this is all that counts?

The World Class Myth

I find it easiest to address these questions in the context of examples from companies I have worked with. The examples that follow illustrate different versions of the myth and their consequences.

Flying High

A handful of aircraft companies compete for the opportunity to build a new airplane. They win when they obtain a large order from a major airline or a substantial contract from a defense agency. Once an aircraft program is won, thousands of people band together for six to eight years to produce a single artifact—an airplane. When they are done and ongoing production is all that remains, they move on to the next aircraft development project. If they are lucky, they can be involved with building three or four airplanes over a thirty-year career, seldom with the same company.

I have worked with a half-dozen commercial and military aircraft companies. They are amazingly insular organizations. People in them have known each other for years. Quite often, these relationships extend across employment in different companies. These people tell a wealth of stories about past aircraft programs. They exude expertise.

They also pay little if any attention to outside expertise and opinions. In one of these companies, a senior manager rejected an idea I proposed by saying, "If it was such a good idea, we would have had it." The key, therefore, is to get people inside the company to have the idea. (If you manage to do that, you run the risk of losing any role at all in the execution of the idea, but it may be your only chance.)

Sometimes this attitude goes too far. I was talking with another senior manager in the same company about the concerns of one of the major airlines in the United States. She said, "Their opinions are not very important to us." This comment epitomizes the arrogance that is often associated with the world class myth.

The feeling of being the best at everything that matters while discounting any external input tends to lay a foundation for later problems. In recent years, all of the aircraft companies with whom I have worked have laid off many thousands of employees. The transition from world class to unemployed can be rapid.

Foreign competition is also intensifying. In commercial markets, the European Airbus consortium was the only competition until recently. It is now likely that there will be one or more East Asian competitors. In military markets, all countries are trying to keep their defense industries alive.

The answer to increased competition is often increased innovation. However, the world class myth is holding the aircraft industry back. If the only ideas that count are the ones you have yourself, your set of alternatives is far too limited. For the new competitors, almost all ideas come from outside, which gives them a much more impressive set to choose from.

New competitors may come from surprising directions. The mature, commodity-like nature of aircraft production makes it very difficult for new entrants. This difficulty can be circumvented by not attempting to become yet another provider of look-alike airframes. Instead, it is much more likely that the real innovations will not involve the airplane itself.

At some point, it is quite possible that the providers of the computing hardware and software on the airplane will subcontract the assembly of the computer cabinet—the airplane—to current aircraft manufacturers. The primary value added will be what computers can do for the air crew, cabin crew, and especially the passengers. As this trend inevitably emerges, aircraft manufacturers will become suppliers. Their world class myth will have undermined their former leadership position.

Changing Faster and Faster

Although there are many computers on aircraft and in use throughout the aviation industry, computer companies are different from aircraft companies. Their product life cycles are measured in months rather than years. To remain competitive with each new product, computer companies have to pack more and more computing power into less and less space.

The result of this competition has been amazing. Computers used to fill rooms, then walls of cabinets, then file-cabinet-sized boxes—and now my laptop is about the size of one volume of an encyclopedia. Further, I have much more computing power at my fingertips than I did with any of the early behemoths.

In the process of working with computer companies, I have encountered many talented people in processor design and packaging, software development, and human-computer interface design. And, as with the aircraft companies, I have often encountered individuals and groups who are totally convinced of the superiority of their own skills.

This world class myth frequently extends to these people's perceptions of their customers. They may, for example, dismiss the fact that customers want benefits in addition to fast processing. For instance, customers usually want compatibility across different computer functions. Those suffering from the world class myth typically question the intelligence of anyone who would sacrifice computing power in order to perform all their work tasks on one computer.

The myth in the case of computers has two elements: (1) a tendency to perceive that you are on top of the heap in terms of the ability to create the fastest processor ever and (2) a sense that this ability is all that matters. The implication is that the market will eventually act rationally and buy the fastest computer—in other words, the best.

Many data now show this assertion to be unwarranted. There is a general consensus that Microsoft bested Apple with inferior technology. The fastest microprocessor in the world—Digital's Alpha—has a minuscule share of the desktop market. Clearly, market success entails more than just having the best technical solution.

However, technically oriented enterprises that have succumbed to the world class myth dismiss any possibility that less than a leading-edge solution can be competitive. Consequently, they accept increased costs and technical risks, as well as increased time to market, in order to create state-of-the-art products that they have difficulty selling. Their technical expertise provides little advantage. In fact, it severely hampers them.

In general, the world class myth makes everybody feel good about themselves and their organization. However, as this example illustrates, even when the myth is close to being true, it is only an advantage when the world class capability provides substantial benefits in the marketplace. If the market doesn't care, the capability doesn't matter.

Pioneering

Large companies are not the only businesses susceptible to the world class myth. I have worked with many small, high-tech companies where the myth dominates the corporate culture. To the extent that the myth overrides important business issues, it can lead to poor performance and potentially to failure.

Typically, these companies are young and have close affiliations with academia. The engineers and scientists at these companies tend to have newly minted, state-of-the-art skills. Hence, they are familiar and comfortable with the leading-edge technologies that many magazines and journals are touting.

With this starting point, such companies are often inventive and quick. Their skills, ambitions, and lack of infrastructure enable rapid progress. At the same time, however, their lack of business acumen—and sometimes outright disdain for it—often leads to difficulties such as cost overruns and slipped schedules.

Sooner or later, these companies tend to encounter problems keeping up with the state of the art, at least with contributions to it other than their own. No longer in the embrace of the university, where the state of the art was digested and packaged for them, they do not keep up with the technical and scientific literature. Nevertheless, the world class myth keeps them feeling that they know everything.

In talking to people in such companies, I have often found that they think every idea they have is pioneering. They create new terms, seldom with crisp definitions. They dismiss other approaches, although they have not studied them. They simply cannot imagine that anyone could devise better solutions than theirs.

I remember talking with one person about her company's supposed world class image. I asked if she did the things that I expected would be associated with this reputation. For example, I asked if she felt on top of related technology development around the country. She said, "No, we don't need to worry about that." Based on this response and others, it was clear that she did not really know whether her company was world class. She had just accepted the prevalent assertion and liked the idea.

World class capability requires knowledge and skills that surpass almost all other participants in the endeavor of interest. To gain this knowledge and achieve these skills, much hard intellectual work is necessary. If you do not have a large proportion of your organization doing such work, the chances are that world class status is truly a myth in your organization. The sooner you can banish this myth, the sooner you can begin to create real organizational strengths that will provide competitive advantages.

Batting 1,000

Private sector enterprises are not the only ones to succumb to the myth of being world class. The public sector can also be trapped by this debilitating delusion. My experiences as a member, and occasionally chair, of advisory committees for numerous government agencies provide ample illustrations.

My first encounter with the blatant pursuit of world class status occurred a few years ago during a briefing at one agency. Members of the advisory committee were providing overview presentations of their assessments of the research being pursued within the technical disciplines their subcommittees were assigned to evaluate. Senior executives within the agency were in the audience.

I was surprised to hear that *every* activity of *every* discipline was world class. Nowhere in the world was anyone doing better research. I was particularly surprised because I knew that our subcommittee's upcoming presentation suggested that one or two areas could be improved. Subsequently, our presentation was silently received, with no questions or comments.

Soon after this meeting, I was called by the agency and upbraided for letting this presentation happen. As the senior member on the committee, I should have known that public criticism was not acceptable. Agency officials suggested that this mistake would threaten current and future budgets.

More recently, I was involved in a review of the programs of a defense agency striving to prove itself to be a world class organization. The review was motivated by an informal comment by a politically appointed assistant secretary. He stated that only world class organizations could avoid being felled by the ax of base realignments and closures.

It was absolutely amazing to see how much activity can be generated by an informal comment. Committees were formed, meetings were held, and numerous debates were targeted at the issue of what "world class" means within the government. Rather than look at results in terms of what the agency was accomplishing, the focus was on status in the sense of whether or not the organization was a world class treasure deserving to be preserved.

The problem in both of these government-related examples is the inability to judge value. The government is partially unable and totally unwilling to judge the value added by each of its organizational entities. The underlying difficulty is the lack of consensus on problems, solutions, and measures for evaluating the benefits provided by all players in the system. As a consequence, much energy is invested in protecting turf rather than adding value.

The focus is on judging inputs rather than outputs. In other words, budgets are evaluated, capabilities are assessed, and organizational performance remains elusive. In this context, world class status is meaningless. Although people in the organization may like the idea, investors—in this case taxpayers—are quite right to be more oriented to the bottom line. Certainly, the time horizon should be far enough away to enable counting both short- and long-term accomplishments. Nevertheless, accomplishments, not status, are what matter.

Regardless of whether your organization is in the private or public sector, you should avoid the delusion that simply being a world class organizational entity is valuable. The key issue is whether or not world class capabilities translate into a demonstrated competitive advantage to win wars, treat diseases, reduce poverty, or simply make profits.

Central Principles

The lessons learned from the examples in this chapter are summarized in Exhibit 2.1. Applying these competency principles will ensure that your organization emphasizes what really matters in terms of knowledge and skills and will help you shift the emphasis from status to competitive competencies.

Exhibit 2.1. Competency Principles.

- World class capability takes much work to achieve; if you are not doing the work to gain and maintain knowledge and skills, your world class status is truly a myth.

- Being the world's best at something is only an advantage when this capability provides substantial benefits in the marketplace; ask yourself whether your world class capabilities really make a difference.

- If the only ideas that count are the ones you have yourself, the set of alternatives is far too limited. Make sure that your organization is open to new ideas from outside the organization.

- The ability to admit and understand your weaknesses can become one of your greatest strengths. Make sure that you openly ferret out weaknesses and constructively remedy these deficiencies.

The examples of aircraft and computer companies illustrate situations in which companies arguably are world class, at least along certain disciplinary lines. For the aircraft companies, this myth keeps them from making the innovations necessary for maintaining market leadership. In contrast, embracing the myth keeps the computer companies from investing in the knowledge and skills necessary for competing effectively.

In these two cases, the companies are not deluded about the skills they claim. They have the skills. The delusion is the sense that these skills are all that matter. These companies have, in effect, chosen to place themselves at a competitive disadvantage—in the near term for computer companies and in the longer term for aircraft companies. Hubris has replaced sound business judgment.

The example of small, high-tech companies illustrates organizations attempting to claim an unjustified status, whereas the examples of government agencies illustrate organizations aspiring to a meaningless status. In these two cases, the myth is truly a myth. The delusion is in the status rather than solely in the value of the status.

Thus, the world class myth involves two delusions. The first concerns the extent to which the organization has the preeminent knowledge and skills that it claims. The second relates to the advantage provided by this preeminence. Both delusions can lead to ruin.

What about companies that are truly world class—companies in which this status does provide strong competitive advantage? My experience in working with such companies is that they have not succumbed to the myth. Despite their obvious expertise, they always seem to feel they are playing catch-up. Although they are confident of their abilities, they feel they have to try harder and harder to keep up with the pace of change.

These organizations also readily admit weaknesses. They try to quickly understand the sources and implications of these weaknesses. Then they find the necessary knowledge and skills wherever in the world they exist. This orientation to admitting and understanding weaknesses is one of their greatest strengths.

Key Questions

The second element of challenging commonly held assumptions involves letting go of the world class myth. Exhibit 2.2 summarizes several key questions that will help you avoid succumbing to the myth. The questions embody the lessons just discussed.

Exhibit 2.2. Letting Go of the World Class Myth.

- Is the general feeling that all functional areas of your organization, as well as your organization as a whole, are outstanding or at least above average? Is this feeling justified?

- Does your organization do the work necessary for achieving and maintaining preeminent capabilities in areas that provide competitive advantage?

- From where do the important ideas in your organization come? What proportions of innovations are coming from customers, competitors, and other industries?

- What processes do you have for identifying weaknesses in your organization, and how well do these processes work?

- What processes do you have for remediating the deficiencies that you identify, and how well do these processes work?

The overall problem with world class status is *not* the competencies implied. Instead, the problem is the attitude engendered and the delusions that result. Insularity and often arrogance lead to disdain for competitors, customers, and ultimately to any idea or desire that is not internally generated. The result is eventual business failure.

We Own the Market
Assessing Relationships with Markets

What is your relationship with the marketplace? How do existing and potential customers view your company? How does your constituency view your organization? Is your thinking aligned with your customers or constituencies, or are you ahead of or behind them?

Most enterprises view themselves as having positive relationships with their markets. They think they are perceived as providing indisputable value. They think they are aligned with their markets—or perhaps even ahead and able to anticipate needs and wants.

Companies with established leadership positions in markets tend to assume that these positions will continue. They seldom do. Douglas Aircraft once dominated the commercial aircraft market. General Motors dominated the automobile market. International Business Machines dominated business computing, and Digital Equipment Corporation dominated engineering computing. All of these companies are still players in their markets, but they no longer dominate. They all went through painful and expensive transitions as they came to recognize that their relationships with their markets had changed. The corporate cultures of some of these companies are still in the process of adapting to these changes.

Our American culture extols being Number One. This status, however, can lead to a critical delusion. You can own a market briefly, maybe for several years. But, you cannot own it permanently. To the extent that owning the market becomes a fixture in your corporate culture, you will inevitably delude yourself and undermine useful strategic thinking.

Unfortunately, this delusion occurs naturally. For all of us, past experiences tend to be compelling and to make us think that the future will be very similar to the past. Consequently, our past successes in providing value to customers make us think we can continue to add the same value in the same way. But customers' needs and desires change; the relevance and competitiveness of our approach to adding value is likely to diminish.

Avoiding this delusion involves constantly monitoring market signals and regularly assessing your relationships with your markets. Signals include straightforward measures such as market size, number of competitors, market share, revenues, gross margins, and net margins. More subtle indicators include the emergence of new technologies and new players, pressures for standardization and consolidation, and customers' reactions to new product releases.

Defining the signals relevant to your market, benchmarking these signals against other companies and other time periods, and regularly assessing your situation are key elements of strategic thinking. Failure to do this can lead to seriously flawed strategies and plans. In *Start Where You Are* (Rouse, 1996), I discuss how this type of failure has led to the demise of many companies.

Let's say that your assessment leads you to conclude that your relationship with the market is faltering. You then have to ask yourself, Why? A good way to address this question is by first considering past successes. What was the situation, in terms of the marketplace signals, when your relationship was strong?

Quite often, I find that people attribute past successes to their having made the right decisions and executed well. Current declines are often attributed to uncontrollable external circumstances. Psychologists refer to this natural tendency as the fundamental attribution error. Put simply, success is always due to great skill, and failure is always due to bad luck.

However, success is more than likely related to being in the right place at the right time. Our business heroes did not make the times. Their skill was in taking advantage of the times. From this perspective, a withering relationship with your market is usually due to your lagging behind the times. The key to improving your situation is to at least catch up with the times and perhaps try to get ahead.

In other words, successful relationships with markets are usually built on making new paradigms work well. There is money to be made milking old paradigms, but only for a limited time. Further, failure to realize what you are doing and its inherent limits can easily lead to the delusion that you own the market.

Assessing Relationships with Markets

Avoiding this delusion involves carefully assessing and interpreting your relationships with markets. In this section, I illustrate the difficulty of this task using examples from automobile, defense, and small high-tech companies.

Assuming That Customers Will Buy Anything

The automobile industry provides a rich set of illustrations of losing track of relationships with markets. General Motors epitomizes this problem. It is amazing that GM could be so confident of its relationships with its markets that they could try to sell a Cadillac that was identical to a Chevrolet except for the nameplate. They asked customers to pay many thousands of dollars for a nameplate that cost a few dollars. Customers balked. Surprise, surprise.

This is but one of many, many examples. One senior GM manager, in discussing design methods and tools, told me that they felt confident in their leadership position in these technologies. One look at GM's products confirms the suspicion that the world class myth is alive and well. This is an example of getting better and better at producing products that the market wants less and less.

A senior manager at a GM auto parts subsidiary commented that his management team was too busy to deal with the real issues. They were focused on operational problems involved with maintaining the status quo. There was no time to assess the longer-term relevance of their market models.

In contrast, my experiences with other automobile manufacturers and suppliers were quite different. These companies were focused on how value would be added to automobiles in the future. A major concern was identifying the intellectual property that is to become the highest-margin element of these automobiles. Not surprisingly, many of our conclusions centered on the new functionality available via electronics and software rather than the value added of forging, casting, and assembly processes.

The U.S. automobile industry lost track of its markets and lost substantial portions of these markets to the Japanese and others. Due to U.S. manufacturers' delusion that they owned the market, it took many years for Ford and Chrysler to recognize their true situation. GM has yet to fully come to this realization. In the process, these companies have lost many billions of dollars.

Counting on Yesterday's Sales

Defense companies are particularly adept at deluding themselves about market relationships. When a defense company has a major production contract, employees act like they own the market. For example, when I worked with McDonnell Aircraft, who had production contracts for the F-15 and F-18 aircraft, and Lockheed, who had the contracts for the F-16 and F-22 aircraft, the overall feeling among employees was that they were indisputable market leaders. Consequently, they perceived situation assessment as a simple matter: you just measure the contract backlog.

There are often lean years, however. New defense procurement dollars have been decreasing for the past ten years. Fewer big wins are possible. Consolidation is rampant. For example, in the past few years, Lockheed acquired General Dynamics' aircraft division, and Martin Marietta acquired General Electric's military electronics division. Lockheed and Martin then merged. They subsequently acquired Loral.

Because it is difficult to grow in a declining market, companies are buying market share. (Of course, others are selling market share and leaving the market.) The acquirers are buying backlog. In this way, they are sustaining their relationship with the market. The result may be that a few large defense companies, in effect, own the market.

At the same time, the U.S. Department of Defense is slowly redefining the market. In the past, the DOD paid for the design, development, and manufacture of virtually everything that went into the weapon systems they bought. This required many engineering and manufacturing person-hours and, consequently, resulted in high costs. In a cost-plus environment, this led to high profits, which were calculated as a percentage of costs. Thus, from the defense company's point of view, the higher the costs the better.

This practice not only inflated costs but it resulted in the DOD's not being able to take advantage of commercial technologies which, in domains like computers, were evolving faster than defense technologies. This led to spending more to buy less. Recognition of this problem led the DOD to change some rules.

The DOD now often specifies the use of nondevelopmental items and commercial off-the-shelf components (referred to as NDI and COTS). In adopting this practice, the department is creating a new relationship with its suppliers. Weapon systems heavily populated with NDI and COTS assemblies and components do not require as much labor as traditional weapon systems. As noted earlier, defense companies' revenues and profits are almost completely determined by the labor content of what they build. Thus, NDI and COTS requirements create strong downward pressures on margins.

This is an example of a relationship changing because of the ways products are produced rather than because the products have changed. Those who can recognize and adapt to this change of processes most quickly will create new relationships and gain new opportunities. For example, one medium-sized defense company won contracts away from a much larger incumbent contractor because it could respond better to NDI and COTS requirements and offer a cost advantage.

The changes being experienced by large defense companies are also affecting medium and small companies in the industry. As the larger companies consolidate, the smaller companies have fewer customers from which to seek subcontracts. The resulting scramble for a share of a declining market precipitates consolidation among these smaller companies.

This scramble is resulting in a few smaller companies becoming larger as they acquire other players. The acquiring companies tend to be very savvy about the defense business and know how to manage contracts and costs closely. The acquired companies are usually much less skilled in these areas. Thus, the ongoing consolidation seems to be good for overall efficiency.

Where is this process headed? Growth via acquisition in a consolidating industry is inherently limited. Continued growth for both larger and smaller defense companies will eventually require diversification. At some point, this diversification will involve non-government markets, which will necessitate new types of relationships with markets. Defense companies have very little experience with these types of relationships.

A major risk is faced by the companies that have successfully gobbled up a variety of other defense companies. They could delude themselves into thinking their knowledge and skills apply unchanged in nongovernment markets. However, owning a declining market—one in which no one else is willing to pay the cost of entry—is very different from competing in markets where continual change prohibits remaining dominant for any extended period. Avoiding this delusion will be key to continued growth for surviving defense companies.

Building Better Mousetraps

Next I focus on delusions about relationships that never existed. High-tech companies, for example, are often founded with a vision of an emerging technology enabling a new product, or occasionally a service, that will create and capture a market. Frequently, such companies are, informally at least, spin-offs from universities. These companies are usually well endowed with technical knowledge and skills, as well as brimming over with market aspirations.

They very seldom, however, have any relationship with the marketplace. A primary goal, therefore, should be to formulate and create the market relationships necessary to taking advantage of their wealth of technological know-how. However, these types of companies usually focus most of their energies on getting the technology to work, both in the product itself and in the manufacturing process.

Market relationships are not ignored, but they rarely get sufficient attention, partly due to a lack of resources and expertise but also due to the mousetrap myth: build a better mousetrap and the world will beat a path to your door. As appealing as this saying is, it is wrong.

I remember a working lunch with several members of our software staff a few years ago. We were talking about how a new technology capability could be marketed, as both a product and a service. Late in the discussion, somebody said, "I don't really understand this marketing stuff. If you have a really great product, people will buy it without having to convince them. The greatness of the product will convince them on its own."

This was not an isolated remark. I could see that many around the table had similar feelings. They sat waiting to hear my reactions. I responded by saying, "You're right. If we had one of the world's truly great ideas, we might be able to create a product that would result in long lines at our door. Unfortunately, we have never had one of the world's great ideas. We just have good ideas that need a little help to become successful products and services."

People did not disagree with me, but they still felt disappointed. The basis for this disappointment is also the basis for small high-tech companies deluding themselves about market relationships, that is, the tendency to accept a very modest amount of evidence as complete confirmation that your product will be wildly successful. Once a few people buy your product, you're likely to jump to the conclusion that everyone will want it.

This success is, at best, only evidence of an emerging relationship with the market. The market in general still does not know who you are and does not have expectations of the value you provide, nor does it have reasons to buy from you. Although it may be possible to judge the merits of your product, the market cannot judge the ability of your organization to provide product support and other services.

My experiences in starting Enterprise Support Systems (ESS) illustrate the necessary evolution in thinking about market relationships. This company became independent after a few years of incubation as a division and later subsidiary of Search Technology. ESS provides computer-based planning systems and related training and consulting services.

ESS's market relationships were initially based on Search Technology's market relationships. Customers, in effect, knocked on the door asking for planning solutions—both software and services. It soon became very clear, however, that strong growth would only come if ESS started knocking on doors.

Once you start doing that, you need something to say when the door opens. We could have said that we were a software company like Microsoft or a consulting company like McKinsey. Instead, we positioned ourselves in the middle of these two industry leaders. We provided enough consulting help to empower customers to solve their own problems via sophisticated planning software.

This positioning avoided the appearance that we were trying to be just like the big players. It also confused potential customers because we did not fit a standard category. Although we argued that we provided the best of these two types of companies, customers sometimes seemed to worry that we would combine the worst of each type.

The solution to this confusion was to carefully design our brochures, mail-out pieces, Web pages, and so forth. All the material now provides a consistent, educational message. The development of success stories with a range of customers was also of great importance. The result was a slow but sure creation of an understandable and appealing image.

The important lesson was how much careful attention this takes. You have to define the type of relationship you want to create and ensure that the market values this type of relationship. You have to create materials—and products and services—that build and reinforce this image.

ESS flirted with the delusion that the market might beat a path to our door. Fortunately, however, our customers have always corrected our potential misperceptions long before they could lead to major problems. Paying careful attention to such existing relationships is a key to learning what new relationships need to be created and how this can be accomplished.

Summary

The examples in this section have illustrated how three very different types of companies have dealt with market relationships. The U.S. automobile companies lost track of what their customers wanted. The surviving defense companies gained relationships via acquisitions but inevitably will face having to develop new relationships in different markets. Small high-tech companies tend to overestimate the extent of their existing relationships and underestimate the time and resources required to create the relationships upon which success depends.

In all of these cases, the result is flawed strategic thinking. Automobile companies tried to get better and better at something they should not have been doing any longer. Defense companies developed long-term strategies that could only work in the near term. Small high-tech companies avoided developing strategies that were central to profitable growth. In all of these examples, the delusion of owning the market was often very costly.

Central Principles

The lessons learned in this chapter are summarized by the relationship principles in Exhibit 3.1. Applying these principles will help you attend to your market relationships.

The delusion of owning the market often reflects a lack of attention to the nature of your relationships with your markets. Paying attention involves determining the signals relevant to your markets, regularly measuring these signals, and honestly interpreting the measurements.

The process of interpretation depends on your abilities to understand your past successes and failures. This involves determining how skill and luck interacted in both successes and failures. Identifying skill deficiencies is key to remedying them. Clarifying the role of luck is key to avoiding delusions about skills.

Assessing relationships often leads to a need, or at least a desire, to change relationships. This may involve changing product or process paradigms, or both. Successful changes require balancing a continued reliance on old paradigms with embracing new ones. In particular, you want to milk the old while you are gaining

---

Exhibit 3.1. Relationship Principles.

- Identify the key signals in your market, benchmark these signals, and regularly assess your situation.

- Avoid attributing all successes to your skills and all failures to your bad luck.

- There is money to be made milking old paradigms, but only for a limited time.

- Avoid trying to get better and better at things you should not be doing at all.

- Long-term success is usually built on making new paradigms work very well.

- New paradigms can affect both your products and the processes used to produce your products.

- Paying careful attention to existing relationships is a key to learning what new relationships need to be created.

skill with the new. You do not have to be the originator of the new paradigm, but you do have to execute very well.

Throughout the process of change, you should pay careful attention to your existing market relationships. The companies and people with whom you have established relationships can provide invaluable feedback as your plans evolve. Their involvement will also help ensure that you do not have to sacrifice existing relationships to establish new ones.

Key Questions

The key to avoiding deluding yourself about market relationships is to pay attention to those relationships. Exhibit 3.2 lists several questions that can help you do this. The questions embody the principles just discussed.

The essence of the delusion addressed in this chapter is *not* whether you really own the market. Instead, the problem is the attitude that results once you are convinced you own the market. When this happens, you stop listening to the market. You stop paying attention and conclude that you know best. At that point, you most certainly no longer own the market. From then on, your assumption is a delusion.

Exhibit 3.2. Assessing Relationships with Markets.

- What signals are key to assessing your relationships with your markets?

- What measurements do you regularly make to assess your relationships?

- What were the real reasons for your past successes and failures?

- What old paradigms are you in the process of abandoning, and what new paradigms are you adopting?

- How are you balancing this parallel abandonment and adoption of paradigms?

- What existing market relationships are key to learning how to develop the new relationships you seek?

Part Two

Establish Goals That Make a Difference

We Have Already Changed
Moving Beyond the Status Quo

I am often involved with helping enterprises formulate new strategies, create plans for new market offerings, and design substantial organizational changes. These efforts usually begin with a discussion of goals. In particular, we focus on the ways in which achieving stated goals will make a difference to the enterprise.

The stated goals are often the same—something like enhanced revenues and profits, increased shareholder value, or improved services to constituencies. Below the surface, however, other goals are often predominant. Achieving these hidden goals will seldom make a real difference.

This chapter and the next four chapters focus on an essential element of successful strategic thinking: establishing goals that make a difference. In the absence of such goals, the results of strategic thinking tend to be plans that keep everybody busy but rarely meet expectations. Instead, underlying, unstated, and usually underwhelming goals are achieved.

In particular, I have found that many companies, as well as other types of enterprises, often pursue planning with the following orientation:

- Planning and commitment become a process of trying to justify the strategic value of what you are already doing.
- Considerable effort is invested in making sure that everyone's current efforts are central to potential new directions.
- New goals and plans do not look very different from old goals and plans, which tends to make everyone feel good about the planning process.

This orientation needs to be surfaced and challenged if real goals are to be established.

This chapter deals with the delusion of already having changed when, in fact, you have simply reinforced the status quo. Subsequent chapters focus on obsessions with technical correctness, the delusion that one big win will solve all your problems, the illusion of having consensus, and the dysfunctional effects of only trying to make the numbers.

Creating Change

Good strategic thinking and planning involve creating change, that is, considering alternative futures, figuring out how these futures might be realized, determining their likely consequences, and either committing to one of these futures or reconsidering the alternatives. Whereas the status quo is often *an* alternative, strategic thinking does not begin by assuming that the status quo is *the* alternative.

If, however, the explicit or implicit goal is to avoid change and maintain the status quo, the activity called planning is actually just budgeting. This activity involves determining how many people, machines, facilities, and so forth are needed to accomplish the same things you have accomplished in the past. While you are likely to aspire to doing these things a bit better, and in the process increase revenues and profits, the usually implicit assumption is that the status quo is to be maintained.

Why does this happen so often? Why is budgeting most often what is really happening when people say they are doing strategic planning? It is due to the here and now—the current way of doing things—being very compelling. Other ways of doing things— alternative markets, products, and processes—are by comparison rather abstract. Alternatives also tend to be expressed, at least initially, in broad terms, leaving many people uncertain about what their specific roles will be if any of these alternatives are pursued.

Consequently, strong underlying forces can make it extremely difficult to escape the status quo. Even though people may find an alternative future intriguing, they also, for the most part, will not know how to create this future. But they know exactly how to maintain the status quo. Thus, their activities tend to reinforce the status quo, even if those activities only serve to keep people busy and feeling productive.

This can result in a debilitating delusion. All the talk and all the meetings of planning teams may be about change. At the same time, however, almost all the activity is likely to be focused on the status quo. With enough talk and enough meetings, people may begin to conclude that change has happened. Yet, almost nothing has happened beyond talk.

The key to avoiding the delusion that change has occurred is the simple recognition that change is not a process of completely rejecting the status quo and embracing all new products and processes. If your only choice is complete rejection of absolutely everything you are currently doing, you have to very seriously question the basic viability of your organization. More realistically, successful change involves carefully preserving selected elements of the status quo while changing many other elements.

The key to avoiding the delusion of change is making these choices explicit. If everyone knows that you are keeping A, B, and C while eliminating X, Y, and Z, it is much more likely that energies will be invested in A, B, and C. This will be most likely if it is clear how A, B, and C fit into the new future and why X, Y, and Z do not.

Making these choices can be difficult. It is often nearly impossible to put a stake through the heart of an idea. Starting new things is much less difficult for most organizations than stopping old things. However, this is precisely what you have to do if you are to avoid the delusion of having changed while, in fact, you are simply maintaining the status quo.

Moving Beyond the Status Quo

To illustrate the delusion of having changed, I discuss in this section several stories that illustrate the very natural ways in which this delusion emerges and how a variety of enterprises have succumbed to or avoided this delusion.

Back to Bologna

Despite the fact that I have been a faculty member at four universities—two in leadership positions and two in one-year visiting positions—academia is an enigma to me. In terms of content (in my case science and engineering), universities tend to be hotbeds of new ideas, often expounded by very talented and impressive free thinkers. As organizations, however, universities are among the most conservative I have encountered.

How can groups of highly educated, mostly liberal intellectuals create such conservative organizations? The organizational structure of disciplinary departments, schools, and colleges is almost sacred, having begun with the founding of the University of Bologna in 1119. The incentive and reward system that totally emphasizes individual accomplishments by faculty members is, in fact, sacred.

As a junior faculty member who made it up through the ranks to tenured full professor, I thought the system was great. There was no doubt about what counted, no doubt about the rules of the game. If you could publish lots of journal articles, bring in sizable amounts of grant money, and earn above-average teacher ratings from students, your success was assured.

However, incentives and rewards that focus solely on creating stars do not necessarily create great organizations. They also do not create institutions that can contribute to the solutions of complex multidisciplinary problems in areas such as education, environment, and health care. What they do produce is students, especially at the graduate level, who are programmed to recreate the standard academic organization wherever they work. This, in turn, makes it difficult for academic organizations to face their own organizational problems.

I have been involved with several attempts at change in academia—attempts usually precipitated by shortfalls (relative to expectations) of externally generated revenues or ratings of educational programs. In one case, state-provided funds were insufficient to cover the costs of undergraduate programs. The department head, seeing no other alternative, was using overhead monies generated by research grants to cover these costs.

I recall a meeting in which the department head asked faculty members to increase their efforts to obtain research grants because he saw the undergraduate shortfall getting worse. The ensuing discussion focused on proposals that might be submitted to federal and state agencies, as well as to private industry. No one asked whether the problem we were experiencing was intrinsic to our current way of doing business.

We left the meeting full of new ideas and enthusiasm. Change was in the air. However, the research topics were all that was changing, not the organization. In fact, we had just agreed on a set of tactics totally focused on preserving the status quo. A lot of midnight oil was burned trying to do our part to avoid change.

The reasons for this result are clear. We were focused on doing what we knew how to do best, that is, on what the incentive and reward system had caused us to learn to do well. We would have been uncomfortable questioning the very foundations of a system in which we had all climbed the ladder of success.

Great Expectations

Serving on advisory committees can provide opportunities to identify delusions because you are not part of the system being evaluated. You are not questioning *your* assumptions and commitments, so it may be easier to identify delusions. However, it often is not any easier to move beyond these delusions.

I have served on, and occasionally chaired, a wide variety of advisory committees. The domains of these committees have ranged from aircraft design to air traffic control to space stations to manufacturing systems to R&D laboratories to university programs. The activities of these committees have included both reviews of ongoing efforts and targeted studies of specific problems or opportunities.

These committees always start with great expectations, at least on the part of committee members, who have been asked to lend their expertise and enthusiasm to an important and interesting endeavor. Members' deliberations and recommendations will have a substantial shaping influence on the future of this endeavor.

Two realities underlie the opening fanfare. In a minority of these situations, the organization that has recruited the advisory committee truly wants an external, objective assessment of some ongoing or planned effort, as well as recommendations on how to improve the effort. But in the majority of these situations, the organization wants the advisory committee to endorse the decisions and actions already taken. They want a report from an august committee that supports the status quo.

This probably sounds devious. It seldom is. The sponsoring organization usually wants insightful reviews and comments. At the same time (typically below the surface) the hope is that the advisory committee will not make waves and rock the boat. The organization hopes to get on with whatever the project is and not have to redirect resources to respond to recommendations.

In this way, committee recommendations are often shaped to ensure that they have a chance of having an impact. Recommendations that would substantially alter directions in, for example, building the space station or upgrading the air traffic control system are avoided. Such recommendations would put the sponsors in the awkward position of having to explain why they do not heed this advice. In the place of these recommendations, a variety of less substantial but much easier to implement recommendations emerge.

Advisory committees are usually populated by intelligent and savvy people. They quickly learn what types of advice are sought and will be valued. They also learn where freedom is limited. The result, not surprisingly, is usually a set of recommendations that matches the sponsor's expectations and that the sponsor typically endorses and implements. The committee members feel good that they had an impact, and the sponsor feels good that the blue-ribbon committee has endorsed its goals, plans, and actions.

In this process, both sponsor and committee create and sustain a substantial delusion. Both parties think they are anticipating and planning for the future. Both think that the advisory committee process creates a balance of internal and external perspectives. This balance, they hope, will result in important yet feasible changes. However, this does not happen.

To illustrate this lack of change, let's consider R&D advisory committees. A typical charge to such committees is to develop a set of goals and long-term plans that will best support the organization's mission. Often, subcommittees or people from within the organization representing different disciplines and functions are available for supporting the advisory committee's work.

It is important to note that as this effort is undertaken, the vast majority of the organization's members are fully absorbed in ongoing R&D efforts. The advisory committee is, in effect, planning for them to be doing different R&D. The advisory committee is basically trying to second guess the R&D staff.

As the committee's work progresses, a hierarchy of goals and plans usually emerges. The question then becomes one of defining the leaves on this hierarchical tree. At this point, someone inevitably asks, "Doesn't Dr. Jones's research on X fulfill need Y?" Similarly, "Can't Dr. Smith's work on A be reoriented to support B?"

Before long, most of the leaves of the tree are labeled with ongoing activities. Some of these activities may have to be slightly reoriented. Some may have to be re-labeled. The bottom line, however, is that much of the status quo will have been endorsed. Some change may have been recommended but much less than appears in the committee's report. The executive summary and hierarchy of goals and plans in this report may cast change in new terms, but the fact is that little change will have been recommended.

This delusion of change is due to a failure to recognize what is really happening. The real role of the advisory committee is to rationalize what is already happening, and perhaps tune it up a bit. This activity is completely reasonable. What is unreasonable is the resulting sense that fundamental changes have been made, or at least recommended. When this happens, organizations think they have already changed and need not further address the need for change. This leaves them unaware and extremely vulnerable.

Filling the Factory

The delusion of having already changed is not limited to academic and government organizations. It also occurs with great regularity in industry. Even though market forces are more evident in industry—and the penalties for ignoring them are more immediate—many companies nevertheless get trapped maintaining the status quo.

The following scenario is common. Competitive pressures from existing and new players in the market, as well as new technologies, lead to the realization that change is needed. For example, quality and service need to be improved while prices are being reduced. In many cases, the functions and features of products need to be reconsidered and substantially revamped.

I have facilitated many planning sessions in which identifying such changes constituted the agenda. In a large proportion of these meetings, it soon became clear that another factor was dominating discussions and decision making—a factor called *filling the factory*. This factor plays a large role in the semiconductor, electronics, computer, communications, and aerospace industries, to name just a few.

Filling the factory involves focusing on strategies, tactics, and plans for maximizing the use of existing manufacturing capacity in hopes of producing the same things that are now being produced. The goal is to take maximum advantage of existing investments. This is reasonable as long as it does not preempt pursuing new directions.

The problem is that it does. Executives and senior managers frequently become preoccupied with operational problems in existing product lines. For example, they spend large portions of their time maintaining major customer accounts. As a result, they spend very little time leading and nurturing new directions. They regularly spend scraps of time discussing new directions. This leads to the delusion that they are pursuing these directions, that they are already changing. Although the organization is totally focused on maintaining, even improving, the status quo, top management thinks they are leading change.

Summary

The delusion of having already changed is ubiquitous. It is a natural phenomenon. The tendency to focus on making the most of existing capabilities is natural. The tendency to keep on doing what you have been doing is natural.

Resistance to change comes in at least two forms. One form is a reaction to uncertainty about what the future holds. The other form is a reaction to the certainty that the future does not hold what you are doing now. Both forms lead, often unconsciously, to the strong inclination to maintain the status quo.

In studies of how change does occur, it has been found that individual champions often emerge and make things happen despite the overall organizational tendencies. In many cases, the champion's quest becomes almost irrational if viewed within the organization's incentive and reward system. The necessity for such inordinate commitments often burns out many champions.

More enlightened organizations foster and support champions. They do this so that their future does not totally depend on irrational commitments made by people willing to operate outside the system. Such people can be invaluable. However, you have fundamental problems if these people are the only ones who can make change happen.

Central Principles

The lessons learned in this chapter are summarized by the change principles shown in Exhibit 4.1. The purpose of strategic thinking

---

Exhibit 4.1. Change Principles.

- Good strategic thinking and planning involve creating change by choosing goals that will truly make a difference.
- The status quo is often *an* alternative. Strategic thinking does not begin by assuming that the status quo is *the* alternative.
- Without goals that make a difference, the results of strategic thinking tend to be plans that keep everybody busy but rarely meet expectations.
- Successful change involves carefully preserving selected elements of the status quo while discarding many other elements.
- Starting new things is much less difficult for most organizations than stopping old things.
- Taking maximum advantage of existing investments is quite reasonable, as long as it does not preempt pursuing new directions.
- Align your incentive and reward systems with the changes you seek. Misalignment will undermine your plans.
- When organizations think they have already changed and need not further address needs for change, they tend to be unaware and extremely vulnerable.

and planning is change, both creating change and dealing with change. If the goal becomes maintaining the status quo, no matter how attractive the status quo may be, your prospects will eventually dim.

Certainly, maintaining the status quo is one of the alternatives you should entertain. However, it is just one alternative, and probably not the most attractive one at that. Growth that is being discussed in terms of the quality of products and services provided, breadth of markets served, and of course revenues and profits should always be prompting consideration of alternatives beyond the status quo.

Such alternatives usually emerge from adopting goals that make a tangible and auditable difference. Goals that cause the enterprise to stretch require careful consideration of elements of the status quo that support the stretch and those that should be discarded. As difficult as it is to discard things for most organizations, this has to happen if you are to achieve stretch goals.

You should take maximum advantage of your existing investments. However, you need to pay careful attention to the costs of taking this advantage. If one of the costs is a resulting inability to pay attention to the new things your organization needs to pursue, then the costs are too high.

As you preserve selected elements of your status quo and discard others, you also need to pay careful attention to aligning your incentive and reward systems with the changes you seek. If your systems are strongly aligned with your past, your future will, at best, look much like your past. And you will have a lot of confused people in your organization.

When you finally feel that you have accomplished change, don't sit back and feel you've made it. What you have achieved is some momentum—the mass of your organization is moving with some velocity. Now you have to keep it moving, which should be easier if you continue to pay attention. However, there is no cruise control in the organizational cockpit. Maintaining momentum still depends on you.

Key Questions

The key to avoiding the delusion of having already changed is paying careful attention to the nature of your goals and making sure

---

Exhibit 4.2. Moving Beyond the Status Quo.

- Are you and your organization committed to goals that will really make a difference?

- What proportion of your organization's resources is focused on maintaining and enhancing the status quo?

- How much time do you spend leading and nurturing new directions?

- What new efforts have you started in the past year? What efforts have you stopped?

- Are your incentive and reward systems aligned with the changes you seek?

- Does your future totally depend on irrational commitments made by people willing to operate outside your organizational systems?

- How do you support champions to work within your systems and succeed?

---

they are not limited to simply maintaining the status quo. Exhibit 4.2 lists several questions that can help you do this. The questions embody the principles just discussed.

The essence of the delusion discussed in this chapter is *not* a matter of whether the status quo has value. Instead, it is the myopic perspective that results when you are convinced that you have already moved away from the status quo—that you have changed. The relative value of the elements of the status quo then becomes unquestioned. At this point, you are trapped by who you are rather than driven by who you want to become. Your delusion is that you have already made it.

We Know the Right Way

Overcoming Obsessions
with Technical Correctness

I often ask executives and senior managers if they have the right expertise in their company to address the problems at hand. Frequently, only half in jest, they say they have too much expertise, or at least too many experts. All these experts think they know the right way.

Organizations highly populated with MBAs, economists, engineers, scientists, lawyers, and other professionals tend to have lots of people who think they know the right way to solve almost any problem. The engineers know how to solve finance problems. The chemists know how to solve political problems. The MBAs know how to solve manufacturing problems.

People who think they know the right way to solve all problems are often obsessed with technical correctness, as defined by their professional discipline. As a result, they can be every bit as oppressive as the advocates of political correctness have been in recent years. Their religious-like fervor seldom allows for alternative points of view.

The difficulty with this mind-set is amplified when several disciplines are involved, which means that several "right ways" are involved as well, many of which may be incompatible. Members of professional disciplines tend to view all problems through their own narrow, disciplinary lenses. They frame problems through these lenses, which appear to dictate particular solutions and involve heavy reliance on the expertise of the person doing the viewing. The inappropriate and inconsistent solutions that result often lead to cross-functional conflicts and counterproductive behavior.

This phenomenon is not at all surprising. Professional education usually focuses on technical correctness, taught by disciplinary specialists with little if any experience or expertise beyond their narrow disciplines. When we hire these newly minted specialists, we house them in functional departments such as marketing, finance, and engineering with other similar-minded specialists. Narrow disciplinary lenses become even more finely focused.

These specialists are eventually asked to address problems that are broader than their specialty. Often they are adept at carving out the portion of the problem that matches their disciplinary skills and declaring that portion to be the essence of the whole problem. In this way, their expertise becomes the critical ingredient in the solution. It becomes particularly interesting when more than one discipline carves up the same problem, as later discussion illustrates.

The key to avoiding such counterproductive situations is to recognize and articulate differences among discipline-specific perspectives and then negotiate compromise positions. This is best done by creating cross-disciplinary teams that, in effect, force different perspectives to converge on a common solution. Although this can be painful for the participants, it can be productive for an organization.

Such teams work best when they have a practical problem to solve that they all agree needs to be solved. Thus, they are not being asked to address an issue in principle; that's when varying disciplinary principles are likely to clash. Focusing on a problem or issue that requires a practical solution or recommendation reduces conflict.

The key insight that participants in such efforts often gain is that no single perspective is correct or right. Instead, each of the differing perspectives provides useful views of the problem at hand; each brings an element of subjectivity to the effort. The confluence of these various subjective orientations can, and often does, lead to creative and useful solutions.

It might be argued that another way to avoid disciplinary biases is to involve only generalists in complex problem solving. The difficulty with this approach is that you need disciplinary expertise to deal with most complex problems. A room full of generalists with no specific expertise can be dangerous.

Groups of generalists can, for example, decide to outsource core competencies because they do not fully appreciate the competitive advantage that such knowledge and skills provide. As another illustration, a state legislature, ignoring basic statistical principles, adopted a resolution asserting that it was the state's goal to ensure that the educational accomplishments of every child in the state would be above the state average.

An equally important reason to avoid teams with only generalists as members is the finding that the best cross-disciplinary problem solvers usually have strong roots in one discipline. The so-called T person has depth in one discipline (the upright stroke of the T) but has broadened to acquire serious interests in other disciplines (the cross stroke of the T). A cross-disciplinary team with several T people as members can be amazingly creative and productive, in part because they avoid obsessions with technical correctness.

Overcoming Obsessions with Technical Correctness

A few examples will illustrate the myth of professional objectivity. These examples show the symptoms of the myth, as well as ways to overcome the impact of one or more groups thinking they alone know the right way.

Functional Silos

Many companies have departments of marketing, finance, engineering, manufacturing, and so on. Typically, people in those departments have certain credentials—degrees, certification, and experience—that are associated with being in the department and that form the basis for their communications with each other. Departments can become insular; members may communicate only with each other. In effect, *functional silos* are formed as peers share common educational and work experiences.

My work with such groups usually involves developing a new, cross-cutting strategy, planning for a new market offering, or entertaining major organizational changes. To address such problems and issues, I always suggest that cross-functional teams be created. Otherwise, the limited perspective of one discipline may dominate.

I recall one planning effort that involved only the marketing professionals in a major aircraft manufacturer. Many of our discussions were dominated by war stories of earlier successes and failures. Everybody knew most of these stories, and the laughter often began when a story was only partially told. Much of my energy was devoted to keeping the group concentrating on the task at hand.

In another planning effort, the group included only engineers and scientists at a government agency. As alternative R&D goals were discussed, the group had a strong tendency to begin the R&D right then and there. At one point, I had to confront the group and ask whether we were going to work on the broad plan for their agency—the task for which we were convened—or whether we would research one of the topics they had raised and perhaps write a journal article before the end of the day.

In yet another effort focused on designing a new generation of microprocessors, the group was dominated by engineers. Our attempts to characterize the market for this processor were frustrating for many members of the team assembled. Finally, one of the more senior team members said, "Can't we just go design and build this thing?" I said he was right. It did not really matter what the market wanted. Fortunately, he reacted by saying it would be ridiculous to adopt that attitude.

The idea of using cross-functional teams to counteract such natural tendencies is hardly novel, but it is surprising how rarely such teams are formed. A recent experience illustrates this. I was working with a cross-functional team at an electro-optics company to develop a strategic plan. The senior managers from marketing, finance, engineering, and manufacturing commented that they had never worked together before. Thinking this comment a bit extreme, I asked if any of them were new to the company or to their positions. They said most had known each other for at least ten years. They frequently golfed together and socialized with spouses.

I then asked, "Do you mean that, in all those years, you never actually had a working meeting together?" They said, "That's right. We never thought to do it. Everybody just did their own jobs." Later, they commented that our three days together had been great, that they now had a much better understanding of what each other did and how the pieces fit together.

Never meeting is certainly an extreme case, but meeting only rarely is common. The natural tendency to interact primarily with disciplinary peers leads to insulated views of the world. It leads to functional silos that often compete for resources and respect. The prosperity of the silo tends to take precedence over the prosperity of the overall organization.

No Respect

I have belonged to several and been involved with many professional societies and associations over the past thirty years. My experiences include a two-year stint as president of an engineering society and a variety of committee assignments in several societies or associations. These experiences have led me to conclude that every discipline thinks it is the Rodney Dangerfield of disciplines: it gets no respect. The first time I heard this complaint, I was motivated to pitch in and help gain more respect. The tenth time I heard it, I began to understand the underlying phenomenon.

Respect, in this context, means being listened to, having your recommendations implemented, and seeing jobs in the discipline preserved. Every discipline thinks other disciplines get too much say and have too much power. Every discipline seems to be seeking parity with other disciplines that have more than a fair share of respect.

To a great extent, this phenomenon is simply an illustration of the grass-is-always-greener syndrome. However, at a deeper level, these perceptions reflect a belief that hard-earned expertise deserves great respect in and of itself. As appealing as this sounds, the truth is that respect is usually more highly linked to the value added by the expertise than to the expertise per se.

The question, therefore, is not whether a particular discipline knows the right way but what value is added by the discipline. Recognition of that fact has prompted many professional societies and associations to focus on collecting success stories and communicating them to their constituencies.

This is a difficult task because success stories in complex domains are rarely attributable to single disciplines. Nevertheless, the process of systematically uncovering contributors to success tends to yield lessons that benefit many stakeholders. It also tends to lead to greater success for the disciplines involved.

This approach to gaining respect also works for cross-disciplinary teams. It is often helpful, when beginning such team efforts, to start by having each discipline explain its lenses, that is, how problems are viewed. These explanations can include success vignettes that illustrate how the different disciplinary views have contributed to tangible successes. This process usually creates an initial foundation of mutual respect and eliminates the delusion that any one discipline knows the right way.

Not Fitting In

The delusion of knowing the right way not only leads to assertions of how problems should be solved but to assertions of how problems should *not* be solved. This latter assertion can sometimes preempt taking advantage of important opportunities that would have provided significant strategic advantages.

A good example of this phenomenon relates to my work in libraries in the 1970s. This work emerged from the confluence of my graduate studies in engineering at MIT and my spouse working in two MIT libraries during this period, and then pursuing graduate studies in library and information science. We were also influenced by the pioneering studies of library effectiveness by Philip Morse, a professor of operations research at MIT.

If you have ever paid attention to the information, reference, or circulation desks in a library, which you tend to do when you are staffing these desks, you immediately notice that one desk may be overwhelmed by patrons, while another may be idle. (If this happens in a grocery store, patrons switch lanes, but in a library the different lanes offer different services.) Watching the ebb and flow of these queues, you cannot help but wonder if there is a way to work out better staffing of these desks.

Of course, this is a standard operations research problem, and there are straightforward ways to optimize staffing. This staffing problem was our first effort in library management. We later studied book circulation, selection of sources for acquiring books, resource allocation across different services, routing of requests in library networks, and the layout of library facilities. These studies were conducted in academic and public libraries in Massachusetts and Illinois.

These efforts resulted in many journal articles, several student projects and graduate theses, and finally a book tying it all together. In all honesty, however, we have to say that we had only minimal impact on the libraries we studied. The many people involved in these efforts hoped that recommendations would be implemented. However, the operations we studied tended to continue as they had before the studies.

What went wrong? In a nutshell, we were devising solutions to management problems that did not fit within the ecology of libraries. Our orientation was economic and technical; the environment was populated by "book people." Their orientation was literary and scholarly.

There was no clash of perspectives. In fact, we worked together quite well and enjoyed our working relationships. However, when the engineering faculty and graduate students went home, the library staff could not adequately explain and defend our efforts. Other staff members' questions or objections tended to derail them.

We tried teaching short courses on our methods, and in one case a full graduate course for credit. The staff members and library science students who attended picked up the material and understood how various models and methods worked. They also gave us very important insights into library operations.

However, their working environments were not conducive to technical-economic lines of reasoning. Diagrams, graphs, and equations were not the currency of these environments. Consequently, despite the promise of benefits in increased efficiency and economy, what we were doing did not fit.

This vignette illustrates two versions of the delusion of knowing the right way. We were deluded in thinking that we had the right solutions to the little technical pieces of the library world we studied. The libraries were deluded in thinking, perhaps only implicitly, that their scholarly and literary model of libraries was inherently the right way to approach managing these institutions.

In the end, we got lots of publications. The librarians felt they had learned many things and enjoyed helping us with our projects.

Yet the gulf between our differing paradigms—perhaps between our similar delusions—was too great to achieve the practical results we sought.

Summary

The examples in this section show how disciplinary lenses affect perspectives on planning and problem solving. Much strategic thinking tends to happen within disciplinary boxes. These boxes only support particular types of goals and strategies. With cross-disciplinary teams, participants can bring their boxes, but only to sit on. Participants need the expertise in their boxes, but only as one ingredient in the cross-disciplinary planning and problem solving required for complex problems.

Central Principles

Exhibit 5.1 summarizes the lessons learned in this chapter in terms of several cross-disciplinary principles. The tendency to identify with one's discipline is natural. Within the insular world of your discipline, your knowledge and skills are extolled. You feel like you belong and are important.

The problem is that you and your peers also tend to develop walls around your disciplinary world. These walls enclose you in a functional silo. Whereas it may be warm and cozy for those inside, such silos hinder the overall organization. The real world—and the real marketplace—is not organized by functions and disciplines. It is organized by human wants and needs. Functional silos cause energy and resources to be diverted from satisfying the markets to satisfying the wants and needs of those in the silos.

Of more importance, functional silos reinforce the importance of disciplinary perspectives. One-dimensional expertise becomes further and further refined. The inevitable result is that each discipline thinks it knows the right way to solve virtually any problem, whether it is internal or external to their discipline.

Fundamentally important is the fact that the various right ways promoted by the different disciplines are seldom compatible. They are not just different views of the elephant. Thus, you cannot simply assemble the different views of a problem and obtain solutions.

Exhibit 5.1.   Cross-Disciplinary Principles.

- The natural tendency to interact primarily with disciplinary peers leads to functional silos that often compete for resources and respect.

- The prosperity of functional silos tends to take precedence over the prosperity of the overall organization.

- The different views of the elephant do not necessarily assemble into anything resembling an elephant.

- Use cross-disciplinary teams to avoid myopic problem solving and decision making.

- Avoid strategic thinking within disciplinary boxes. Members of cross-disciplinary teams can bring their boxes, but only to sit on.

- Identify and articulate differences among discipline-specific perspectives and negotiate compromise positions.

- The confluence of various subjective orientations can, and quite often does, lead to creative and useful solutions.

- Respect is usually more highly linked to the value added by expertise than to the expertise itself.

- A room full of generalists with no specific expertise can be dangerous.

Using cross-disciplinary teams is the key to avoiding the myopic problem solving that underlies the delusion of knowing the right way. A healthy mixture of people from marketing, finance, engineering, manufacturing, human resources, sales, and so on can quickly diffuse the tendency toward disciplinary correctness. Strategic thinking then can occur outside of disciplinary boxes.

Disciplinary expertise is important. You want this expertise brought to bear on the problems of interest. At the same time, you need a process that identifies and articulates differences among discipline-specific perspectives. The best solution inevitably lies in compromise among perspectives.

An important insight is that all perspectives are inherently subjective, at least in the sense that each is based on the choice of a particular set of lenses for viewing problems. This insight leads to the recognition that creative and useful solutions reside at the confluence of the various subjective orientations—at the intersection of differing disciplinary points of view. In this way, the respect accorded a discipline is more highly linked to the value added to this confluence than to disciplinary expertise itself.

The difficulty of balancing points of view and finding a confluence of perspectives can lead management to want to keep experts in the back room. The idea is to use these people as resources but let the generalists tackle the important and controversial problems. This can be dangerous and lead to more than just biased conclusions that single disciplines tend to yield. It can lead to solutions that are physically and logically impossible. Strategic thinking benefits from knowledge and skills. The trick is to avoid having only one set.

Key Questions

The key to avoiding the delusion of knowing the right way is to ensure that multiple perspectives on problems are considered and balanced. Exhibit 5.2 lists several questions that can help you do this. The questions reflect the principles just discussed.

**Exhibit 5.2. Overcoming Obsessions
with Technical Correctness.**

- Does your organization tend to focus on finding the right way, or are multiple points of view encouraged?
- What disciplinary lenses most affect your organization's decision making?
- What functional silos are scattered across your organizational landscape?
- Do you convene and empower cross-functional teams to tackle important problems?
- How do expertise and accomplishments affect earning respect in your organization?

The essence of the delusion discussed in this chapter is *not* a matter of whether disciplinary knowledge and skills have value but the one-dimensional solutions that result when one discipline is convinced it knows the right way—and prevails. Worse yet are situations in which multiple disciplines each think they know exactly what should be done. The delusion is that any one perspective can possibly embody the right way.

We Just Need One Big Win
Avoiding Chasing Purple Rhinos

What single event could make or break your company? Many people answer this question by explaining a potential "must win" project or by outlining the possibilities for a new "killer" technology. If these events were to take place, they say, the company would be set forever. Money would flow in over the transom, and the company stock would soar.

People who answer in this way are, or have the potential to become, purple rhino hunters. Purple rhinos are extremely rare—almost as rare as single events that completely assure a company's future. However, a purple rhino is occasionally found. The rhino (opportunity) is slaughtered, and the corporate village gets to feast and celebrate the company's great foresight and skill.

Within a corporate fortnight, the opportunity has been consumed and the purple rhino hunters head back to the veld. They need to repeat their serendipitous encounter of the rarest of the rare. Everyone waits in anticipation, totally absorbed by waiting. Lesser rhinos wander freely through the village, unpursued and unharmed.

People and organizations often hope that the big win will solve all problems and create prosperity for everyone. Usually the big win does not happen. Explanations usually center on uncontrollable external circumstances. Budgets are cut and people are dismissed. Marketing and sales feverishly try to line up another big one.

When a big win does happen, it is usually due to something other than the company's skills and abilities. Nevertheless, the accepted wisdom is that great plans and flawless execution prevailed.

The victory brings more credibility to the fundamentally self-limiting strategy of hunting endangered species.

However, sustainable success comes from doing many smaller things well and moving beyond an infatuation with big deals. It requires creating a portfolio of lesser opportunities that, as a whole, will ultimately be more profitable than any single big win. Sustainable success comes from understanding and nurturing the many value-added relationships required for one small win after another.

This can be easier to say than to accomplish. Many marketing and sales organizations are solely populated by big game hunters. An occasional big win also creates more excitement than frequent small wins. However, achieving your goal of building a valuable company requires that you forsake feast-and-famine economics.

Avoiding Chasing Purple Rhinos

Defense companies, large and small, are obvious examples of purple rhino hunters. Builders of cathedrals, power plants, and airports are also good examples. Consulting and project-oriented work also provide good illustrations. In this section, I elaborate on these and other examples. I also discuss how the purple rhino syndrome emerges in a wide range of organizations.

Hunting Big Game

Defense companies are particularly susceptible to the purple rhino syndrome. They are completely specialized for rhino wooing. They do not use guns. They use viewgraphs and briefings, which are punctuated by lunches and dinners. The entree is usually a hefty proposal whose value is measured in pounds rather than clarity. Rhinos typically wilt and surrender in the face of this assault.

In the defense business, a good example of a purple rhino is an aircraft production contract that will keep 50,000 workers busy for ten years and ensure many billions of dollars in revenues and many millions in profits. Although there may be numerous lesser rhinos grazing on the defense veld—and hence much potential revenue—the purple rhino gets all the attention. Quite simply, such big wins are the only way to keep 50,000 people productively employed with only one sale.

I recall an initial meeting with one of the major U.S. defense contractors. My task was to help them develop a new strategic plan. I started by asking, "Can I assume that your current plan is primarily a list of government procurements over the next three to five years and your strategy for winning these contracts?" The director of planning responded, "That would be wonderful!"

Their actual "plan" turned out to be a network of relationships and potential deals that their sales force was pursuing. Many of these deals involved foreign military sales where the profit potential is much greater. To make their numbers each quarter, they tried to get one or more of these deals to close. Then, it was on to the next deal. There was no real plan except to close deals wherever they could be found.

This approach to strategy is common. A major U.K. defense contractor with whom I worked said that the company found foreign military sales attractive for more than just the profits. Many of the countries that bought their weapon systems never used them, not even for training exercises. Within a few years, these systems became inoperable due a lack of maintenance and use. The defense contractor could then sell the same weapons to the same customer again.

Not only do purple rhinos dominate defense companies' strategies—or lack of strategies—they also dominate tactical decisions. For example, I was working with a military aircraft manufacturer to develop new ideas for aircraft cockpits. The day it was announced that this manufacturer had won a major new fighter aircraft contract was the day the project I was pursuing ended. All attention and all key personnel immediately shifted to carving up the purple rhino. The planning horizon for this company immediately contracted to just the other side of the downed rhino.

Defense companies provide wonderful illustrations of the purple rhino syndrome, but they are only one example. Companies that build air traffic control systems, nuclear power plants, major bridges, and other types of modern-day cathedrals are also examples. The economic appetites of these organizations are such that purple rhinos seem to be the only answer. As a result, such companies are ill-fitted for pursuing any other kind of game. Defense companies, for example, that try to move into commercial markets almost always stumble. The production staff of defense companies have the know-how to manufacture or fabricate many things. However, the marketing and sales staff—the hunters—are seldom equipped to understand commercial markets and to see how they can make their numbers by making many smaller sales.

Perhaps large defense companies must necessarily limit their attention to purple rhinos. The size of their infrastructure and resulting overhead costs dictate that they either find gargantuan contracts or fade and die. However, the purple rhino syndrome also affects many small and medium-sized companies that would seem to be sufficiently nimble to avoid this trap.

Chasing Rhino Parts

There is a vast network of small- to medium-sized defense companies that seek subcontracts from the large defense companies, as well as contracts directly from the Department of Defense (DOD). Declining defense budgets have threatened many of these companies to a greater extent than the large companies. While the large companies have downsized, many of the smaller companies have simply disappeared. Discussing this trend, I commented to one audience, "When the redwoods tremble, the ferns face disaster."

The smaller companies would seem to have more alternatives than the large companies. They do not have vast manufacturing plants and many layers of infrastructure. So why don't they just reinvent themselves for other markets where growth is possible? Why don't they convert to commercial markets or at least diversify?

The simple answer is that they are too busy chasing rhino parts. They are too busy trying to win the subcontract to produce the sub-gizmo on the XYZ Feathernester. If they win this subcontract, they will be in great shape for three years. If not, they will file for Chapter 11. It all depends on this one deal.

One chief executive of a small defense company told me that he reads the paper first thing every morning to see if they are still in business. A congressional hiccup or a lingering continuing resolution and he is out of business. When I asked him what he was doing about this situation, he said his company was scouring the defense market for similar contract opportunities.

Even though this vignette is representative, some small- to medium-sized defense companies have made the transition to commercial markets. They had strong leadership and commitment from top management. They developed new marketing and sales strategies and tactics, which usually required hiring all new marketing and sales personnel. They knew it would be difficult to retread purple rhino hunters.

Several of the smaller defense companies with whom I have worked focus on R&D contracts directly from the DOD or on subcontracts from the large companies. Many of these efforts involve, in effect, the early stages of creating purple rhinos. The technology developed through this R&D may lead to much larger contracts in subsequent years.

The small- to medium-sized companies are usually the innovators in these efforts. The large companies' involvement is intended to provide contextual knowledge to the smaller companies. Their involvement also assures that these larger companies gain knowledge and skills in the new technologies and hence are receptive once these technologies have matured.

Just as little R&D contracts, if successful, beget larger R&D contracts, little R&D companies tend to lead to larger R&D companies in search of larger projects. However, very large R&D projects are, in themselves, purple rhinos because they are so rare. Nevertheless, I have repeatedly seen larger R&D companies focus almost solely on these larger opportunities, often ignoring much of their traditional business in the process.

Thus, even small and highly agile R&D companies get ensnared by the purple rhino syndrome. It is a natural psychological and sociological phenomenon. It is difficult not to focus on the big prize, despite the abundance of readily available, lesser prizes. It is also great fun to discuss, scheme, and plan how to make the big win, as well as envision the attributes of subsequent success.

Defense companies, large and small, provide compelling, and perhaps classic, illustrations of this phenomenon. However, other types of enterprises are far from immune to it. This delusion is pervasive. A wide range of organizations try to seek one big solution— a panacea for all their problems rather than a series of small solutions.

Hunting Billable Hours

Consulting companies and other project-oriented service companies provide another excellent illustration of the delusion that one big win will solve all problems. Many of these companies regularly experience the feast-and-famine consequences of rhino hunting. When a big project is landed, people swarm the opportunity in search of billable hours.

A senior executive at a major international company told me, "Even the best consulting company is only six months away from being out of business." Even big projects tend to be relatively short in duration. Projects can end at a moment's notice when customers become dissatisfied or change directions.

The competition is intense, in part because the cost of entry in the consulting business is so low—just the price of business cards and stationery. As evidence, the *New York Times* in the early months of the Clinton administration reported that over 5,000 consulting companies had announced health care as one of their areas of expertise. It is pretty easy to announce that you are an expert.

Thus, in the consulting business many people are feverishly looking for big wins. They are trying to find projects that will keep five to ten consultants—or many more—fully billable for the next year or more. They also try to grow projects into bigger and bigger efforts, generating more and more billable hours. In this way, they may be able to convert a run-of-the-mill rhino into a bona fide purple rhino.

Consulting companies have a variety of marketing and sales strategies. A senior partner at one large U.S.-based consulting company told me, "We wait for the phone to ring. Whatever the caller wants, that's the business we are in." A high-ranking partner at another large consulting company said, "A primary source of business is following around another major consulting company and cleaning up the messes they make."

Some consulting companies, and industry practices within consulting companies, have found another way to succeed. They develop long-term relationships with customers and take on a series of small projects, making sure that customers gain much value for each project. This tends to result in a steady stream of revenue from the customer.

Thus, there is an alternative to chasing purple rhinos. You can carefully and patiently build a portfolio of long-term relationships, each of which provides regular if not spectacular revenues. This requires particular attention to customers' needs and preferences, as well as substantial quality control. It is worth it, however, because in the long run it provides more stable and profitable growth.

This strategy seems so obvious, why don't more consulting companies pursue it? The difficulty is the care and patience it requires, as well as the time it takes to result in a steady stream of revenues. This strategy does not solve big problems quickly. It does not create billable hours for ten or more consultants at once. Put simply, this strategy requires a lot more strategic thinking than many consulting companies exhibit. The delusion of needing just one big win tends to get in the way of such thinking.

Summary

The purple rhino phenomenon is not unique to companies that design and develop big systems such as aircraft and power plants, or to companies that go from project to project. I have seen this delusion at work in industries ranging from semiconductors to electronics to computers, as well as in government agencies and nonprofit organizations.

In the computer industry, for example, Apple thought that the Newton (envisioned as a portable digital assistant) would give them the big win. Digital pinned its fortunes on the Alpha chip. On the software side, many companies are hoping that they have the next killer application to follow word processors, spreadsheets, presentation packages, and desktop publishing.

This natural tendency is hard to overcome. However, businesses and other enterprises are best built brick by brick rather than by big wins. Occasional purple rhinos are fine if they wander into your back yard. But you should not sit in the back yard waiting for them. Spend your time laying bricks.

Central Principles

Exhibit 6.1 summarizes the lessons learned in this chapter in terms of several portfolio principles. The key to success is not one big win, not one mega deal. The key is a continual series of small wins.

Big wins create victory feasts and huge bonuses. However, big wins are not sustainable. There simply are not enough opportunities. Thus, the long-anticipated big win usually does not happen.

In the meantime, as the organization holds its breath in anticipation, strategic thinking gets shelved. Plans are not developed for adding value to the market in a step-by-step manner. The organization, stuck on hold, stagnates.

Exhibit 6.1. Portfolio Principles.

- It is a pervasive tendency to seek one big solution—a panacea for all your problems—rather than a series of small solutions.

- People and organizations often hope that a "big win" will solve all problems and create prosperity. Usually the big win does not happen.

- The delusion of needing just one big win tends to get in the way of strategic thinking.

- Sustainable success comes from doing many smaller things well. It involves moving beyond infatuation with big deals.

- Achieving your goal of building a valuable company requires that you forsake feast-and-famine economics.

- Create a portfolio of appropriately diverse opportunities so that success does not depend on frequent occurrences of rare events.

- Carefully and patiently build a portfolio of long-term relationships, each of which provides regular if not spectacular revenues.

- Businesses and other enterprises are best built brick by brick, rather than via opportunistic big wins.

To build a valuable company, you have to forego the feast-and-famine economics of purple rhino hunting. Instead, you need to create a portfolio of diverse opportunities. The goal is to avoid dependence on frequent occurrences of rare events. Such dependence guarantees eventual failure.

A central aspect of creating this portfolio involves focusing on building long-term relationships, which requires care and patience. However, it produces regular if not spectacular revenues. It produces revenues linked to consistently adding value for customers rather than leveraging a rare and fleeting advantage.

Avoiding the delusion of only needing one big win requires recognizing that businesses and other enterprises are best built one step at a time rather than by opportunistic big wins. Even though big wins occasionally happen and can help an enterprise prosper, it does not make sense to count on such events happening with any regularity. Such a strategy is only a bit more reasonable than investing in lottery tickets.

Key Questions

The key to avoiding the delusion of only needing one big win is to recognize the fleeting nature of such remedies. Exhibit 6.2 lists several questions that can help you do this. These questions reflect the lessons just discussed.

The essence of the delusion discussed in this chapter is *not* a matter of whether purple rhinos are valuable. Instead, it is the extreme lack of business prudence that results when your predominant strategy focuses on stalking members of endangered species. You are guaranteed to fail eventually.

You need to create a portfolio of diverse opportunities that relate to each other in terms of your core competencies and the ways in which these competencies add value for your customers. These opportunities need to be integrated with relationships that are, or have the potential to become, long term and sustainable. With this basis, purple rhinos will become fortuitous interludes in the brick-by-brick process of building a real business.

Exhibit 6.2. Avoiding Chasing Purple Rhinos.

- How often have you found your organization depending on a purple rhino to solve all its problems?

- How often have purple rhinos solved any of your fundamental problems, as opposed to simply masking them for a while longer?

- How many of your current business opportunities can be characterized as endangered species—unlikely to contribute to repeatable, sustainable revenue?

- How diverse is your portfolio of business relationships and opportunities? Are there numerous ways to succeed?

- How careful and patient are you in developing and sustaining business relationships via clear and frequent value added?

We Have Consensus
Managing Conflicts of Values and Priorities

Some organizations place great emphasis on reaching consensus on major issues and decisions. I once asked an executive in one of these types of organizations how much time it took to achieve consensus. She responded, "All of it!"

Looking for a more specific answer, I asked how she felt the effort broke down among building consensus, maintaining consensus, and executing the decisions and plans emerging from consensus. She said that in many cases, the first two activities consumed all the time available. They were never able to get to execution because the consensus was so fragile.

What is consensus? It is commonly misperceived as synonymous with reaching complete agreement. However, consensus is only an agreement to act, not necessarily agreement on all the actions to be taken. Consensus is much easier to achieve when viewed as no more than an agreement to move forward despite unresolved differences concerning the relative merits of alternative actions.

Agreeing to move forward, despite differences, is often based on the need for more data to resolve differences. Disagreements about what the market wants, what elements of a solution will work best, and potential consequences of decisions are, in many cases, only resolved by implementing an initial decision and observing the results. Hence, the agreement to act—the consensus to move forward—is the only way many differences can be fruitfully addressed.

The quest for the other version of consensus, that is, agreeing on everything before acting, tends to result in differences being buried. In an effort to get things going or to avoid derailing existing momentum, people often shy away from surfacing perceptions and opinions that contradict the current flow of information and decision making.

Sometimes people's contradictory perceptions are correct, but the organization does not benefit from the early warning that would have been possible if disagreements had surfaced. Instead, the incorrect perceptions are finally set right by the unfolding of undesirable consequences. People are likely to say later, "If only we had known earlier!"

If consensus is achieved by avoiding underlying disagreements, then consensus becomes a delusion. The key to avoiding this delusion is to address these disagreements. By exploring alternative and conflicting views, eventual decisions can be much stronger.

It is often valuable to spend a bit of time being your own worst enemy, the rationale being to focus on finding all the weaknesses of your plans rather than first hearing about them from the marketplace or other constituencies. In this way, you are prepared to deal constructively with criticism.

Broadly speaking, two types of disagreements are of interest. The first involves disagreements about facts. For example, there may be multiple perceptions of the likely market response to a new product or service. This type of disagreement can be resolved by collecting data. Thus, a consensus decision may be to move forward and, for instance, perform a market test.

The second type of disagreement concerns differences, perhaps even outright conflicts, based on deeper roots than varying perceptions of facts. Below the surface of many conflicts about, for example, goals, strategies, and plans are underlying conflicts of values, priorities, and interests. There may be differences of basic needs and beliefs, differences in priorities in meeting needs and supporting beliefs, and differences in vested interests.

These types of differences can stop organizations dead in their tracks. However, exposing and exploring differences can provide a basis for negotiating win-win resolutions of conflicts that would otherwise undermine progress. This involves determining the sources and causes of differing positions on goals, strategies, and plans.

Typically, you can uncover differing needs and beliefs about customers, service, technology, innovation, and so on. For example, you may discover that the engineering people in your organization need technology to be your critical competitive advantage and firmly believe this is the case. Marketing and finance, to name just two other areas, are likely to need something else.

Consequently, engineering may advocate a high-tech alternative for the next proposed product, while marketing may advocate a lower-tech alternative, along with spending more on advertising and promotion; finance may push for higher prices. This should not be surprising, as people's needs and beliefs affect what knowledge they gain, what facts they seek, and how they interpret both.

In *Catalysts for Change* (Rouse, 1993), I elaborate two principles for finding a win-win situation among such differences. First, for the near term, modify alternatives, or find new alternatives that meet needs and do not conflict with beliefs. Second, for the longer term, modify situations (for example, through training) so as to cause a constructive evolution of needs and beliefs.

For example, you might create a win-win for engineering, marketing, and finance by choosing the lower-tech alternative but adding a high-tech component to advertising and promotion using an Internet home page, while charging for services that had previously been free. Your longer-term plan might include upgrading to the higher-tech alternative, offering it in part by the then-mature Internet presence, and charging for new high-value-added on-line services.

The key to avoiding the delusion of having consensus is simply to address disagreements and differences directly. The lack of consensus can actually be a strength as you attempt to refine your goals and plans and ensure that they can pass muster. Searching for win-win solutions amidst disagreements and differences usually results in much better strategic thinking.

Managing Conflicts of Values and Priorities

The delusion of having consensus (in the sense of having agreement about everything) is common in many types of organizations. It is most obvious, however, in non-business organizations where it is not possible to focus on a small set of products or services. The vignettes in this section are drawn from these organizations to make this type of delusion clear. I discuss the phenomenon in business organizations later.

Avoiding Disagreements

I have been heavily involved in a wide variety of volunteer organizations for many years. Examples include professional societies, churches, and charitable agencies. In some cases, I was the elected leader; in others, I was a consultant helping with strategy and planning.

These organizations are "volunteer" in the sense that most of the participants voluntarily affiliate with them and receive no monetary compensation. In contrast, for neighborhood associations and community organizations, which I discuss later, membership is automatic because of where you live. Larger volunteer organizations also include paid staff members. Staff usually run an organization, with considerable latitude, in accordance with the policies of a board of directors whose members are senior and seasoned volunteers.

Organizations like this often face leadership problems. The volunteer officers change every year or two. The senior staff has to avoid being seen as too vigorously filling this leadership void, lest the organization be seen as "staff driven," which could generate conflict. Thus, even though the senior staff may have the pulpit—literally or figuratively—they can't really take charge.

Such organizations often try to manage by consensus. If they can get everybody to agree about goals and plans, staff members can execute the resulting action plans. The key question is how to reach such agreement without some of the volunteers becoming disenchanted and departing.

It is important to recognize that people seldom volunteer without a reason. They are usually concerned with particular issues and programs. For example, a reason for volunteering in a health-related organization may be having a parent or child who suffers from a particular ailment. Volunteering for a church organization may be precipitated by some personal trauma and a desire to help with programs related to that trauma. Volunteers can have very focused agendas.

An organization may be populated by volunteers with a wide variety of agendas competing for scarce resources, including money, facilities, and particularly, staff time. In order to make tangible and substantial contributions to pursuing its mission, the organization needs to focus resources and achieve critical mass in a few high-payoff areas. However, this inevitably means foregoing some current activities, all of which have a constituency.

How can such organizations achieve the consensus they seek? Three ways are common, each of which has very different consequences. First, the organization can adopt goals and develop plans that are sufficiently broad that almost unanimous agreement can be reached. For example, I was involved with one church organization that adopted community and connectedness as their only goal. It was hard for anyone to disagree with this goal. As a consequence, there was a delusion of consensus. However, the church's scarce resources did not become more focused, and underlying differences were submerged rather than addressed.

The second approach is to avoid top-down goal setting, other than at a broad, abstract level. Instead, let new goals, plans, and activities emerge bottom-up. For the few things that survive the Darwinian struggle, broad support and eventually consensus are likely to emerge as a reaction to success. To illustrate, I recently asked the top staff executives in a major health-related volunteer agency how to best get innovations adopted in the organization. In contrast to the official approaches described in their policies and procedures, they suggested the following steps:

- Gain the support of a few key opinion leaders.
- Articulate a clear and simple message.
- Create a targeted success story.
- Do *not* ask permission.

Put simply, go do it. If you succeed, your innovations will eventually gain supporters and be adopted more broadly. This approach basically avoids seeking consensus until it emerges on its own.

The third approach is the most risky. It involves addressing the conflicts underlying the delusion of consensus, that is, exploring the needs and beliefs that form the basis of the differing positions on the issue at hand. This is risky because it may expose a fundamental rift in the organization—a difference in needs and beliefs so basic that win-win solutions are not possible.

I have never experienced such unresolvable situations. Whenever people have been willing to explore underlying needs and beliefs, there have always been ways to create win-win solutions. One approach, for instance, is to expand the scope of the discussion to enable trade-offs across more issues. This often results in concessions that are of great value to one set of stakeholders but of little concern to others. A few concessions of this type make it easier to deal with more thorny issues.

These three approaches to dealing with consensus are very different in philosophy. The first approach—staying at a high enough level that no one disagrees—creates a delusion of consensus. The second approach—Darwinian survival of bottom-up initiatives— avoids seeking consensus but results in the inefficiency of investing in many things for only a few to survive. The third approach— exploration of the basis of conflict—seems to be very risky but can result in much stronger and truly innovative organizations.

Reaching Fragile Agreements

Suburban subdivisions and condominiums often have owners' associations that govern the common property of the group of owners. Owners are automatically members of such associations. Along with full voting rights, members also gain the responsibility to pay their shares of the costs of whatever the group as a whole decides to do.

I was once the president of an association and have been a member of others. My first experience was in a condominium mainly populated by wealthy widows and elderly couples. I bought my condominium as a result of "fire sale" prices during the recession in the mid-1970s. I quickly realized that I was at the very bottom of the economic ladder in the building.

Everyone was very cordial and wanted the small, newly formed community to work. However, conflict soon emerged. Several of the wealthy widows wanted the building staff members to provide many services, such as changing light bulbs in their apartments. They also wanted somebody to chat with. Changing light bulbs became a time-consuming task.

Staff members were happy to be of service, in part because of generous tips and other gifts. The problem was that the work they were being paid to do was not getting done. This problem festered, and our happy little family became less and less happy. The delusion of consensus was finally overcome.

The solution was remarkably simple. Policies were set forth regarding exactly what services owners should expect as part of their association fees. All other services had to be contracted directly with staff members and performed during their off hours. Because those desiring such services were among the most wealthy in the building, they easily agreed to the increased out-of-pocket costs.

The nature of the solution was so simple and the potential for the conflict so obvious, the question arises: Why hadn't these policies been formulated much earlier? That is because such policies could not emerge in an environment with shared expectations of consensus—shared expectations that we would all agree on everything. Everyone dearly wanted this type of consensus, but that was unrealistic. When the bubble eventually burst, it caused everyone stress. The stress levels would have been much lower if we had accepted conflict as an integral element of community and developed mechanisms to manage it. However, the expectation of complete agreement led to exactly the opposite.

A more recent experience involved an invasion of beavers in my lakeside neighborhood. Actually, it was just a few, very efficient beavers who began to systematically clearcut back yards along the lake. The result was emergency meetings with state conservation officers and strategy meetings in neighbors' homes.

Provisioned with pots of coffee and a variety of desserts, we discussed how to counter the assault. A staff member from our local nature center had told us that the male beavers were the main problem. He said, "Let them mate and eat. Then, they'll leave." One neighbor suggested that this advice would work with the males of any species.

We discussed guns, bows and arrows, and traps. Two men tried to shoot the beavers, resulting in wasted bullets and neighborhood children in tears. Somebody set traps, catching one beaver and several dogs and cats. Trees kept on disappearing.

Many people argued that we should do nothing. "The beavers were here long before us," they said, "as were the ducks, geese, turtles, fish, heron, and snakes." Those supporting this view put wire mesh around the trees beavers relish most. They lost no trees.

Soon all the houses had wire mesh on their trees. Beavers still occasionally take a tree of two but in general have retreated upstream or downstream of our lake. The guns, bows and arrows, and traps are all put away. New beaver jokes quickly make their rounds in the neighborhood.

When the assault first happened, we tried to reach consensus. In using the traps, we thought we had reached agreement. However, the neighbors' guns shattered that delusion, as well as my little girl's dreams. In the end, the advocates of peaceful coexistence prevailed by showing how the solution worked in their own back yards. Consensus emerged around a successful solution rather than as a result of an explicit agreement.

Helping Henrietta

During two recent summers, I lived with my family in a small New England town on the Atlantic sea coast. Besides providing a welcome relief from the summer heat of Atlanta, it is a good place to write and recreate. I began this book there. These summers also provided an opportunity to observe the life of this relatively tight-knit community.

One evening, we decide to take in the School Committee meeting. The committee was hearing a proposal for a privately funded "Eco-Farm" on school property that would serve as a learning center for the school and community.

It would seem that whether to accept private donations of over $1,000,000 to create a learning center on idle property would be an easy decision. The stakeholders didn't agree. The homeowners bordering the property were concerned about traffic, about the likelihood that the farm would become a teenage lovers' lane in the wee hours, and about how the farm might destroy the current "natural" state of the property.

The school board decided to table the issue pending satisfactory answers to the questions raised. The advocates of the farm then conducted a series of informal meetings (actually morning coffees and afternoon teas) to discuss these questions with those who had raised them. A professional ecologist, for instance, explained how the current natural state of the property was not at all natural but simply the result of many years of junk shrubs and trees growing over the trash that had been thrown there. The farm would restore much of the vegetation that was natural for the area.

Slowly but surely, the advocates explored the needs and beliefs underlying people's questions and concerns. In this way, some concerns disappeared. Others, such as worries about traffic, remained. However, the bordering homeowners progressively became members of the advocacy team as they found that they were provided a voice in what was happening. This is a good example of how patiently exploring the basis of conflicts can lead to creative win-win solutions.

Here is another example. The town's weekly newspaper came out on Thursdays. One week, the front page was dominated by a large picture of a chicken. The article reported on that week's meeting of the Board of Health. The highlight of the meeting was a complaint by the neighbors against the owner of Henrietta, the chicken. The complaint centered on Henrietta's clucking during the neighbors' dinner hour. They said the clucking was so loud that they could not hear the classical music they liked to play while eating dinner.

There was no ordinance banning chickens per se. However, there was a generic ordinance regarding nuisances. Henrietta, it seemed, was in trouble. The tide turned, however, when Henrietta's owner took the stand and told a sad story. She told of how the chicken had been her father's best friend. Her father and Henrietta, according to the daughter, had both been ham radio operators, a pastime that Henrietta seemed to miss since the old man's death. Henrietta was all the daughter had left to remember her father by. She pleaded for the right to keep the chicken.

Discussion then focused on how long chickens live, the extent to which they can be trained, and so on. Finally, the Board of Health reached a decision. They voted that Henrietta must become an indoor chicken. Daily outings were allowed between 10:00 A.M. and 1:00 P.M. This Solomon-like ruling ended the dispute. Everyone's needs seemed to have been met, and a delusion of consensus emerged.

However, the saga of Henrietta the chicken was not over. Later that winter, I was nearby on business, and I stopped for a cup of coffee with one of our friends. In discussing many odds and ends, I asked how Henrietta was doing. Had she been able to adapt to the life of an indoor chicken?

My friend explained that in the six months or so since Henrietta had dominated the front page of the newspaper, chickens had taken on a higher level of significance for the town. Many women were buying chickens to show support for Henrietta's owner. This had led to the emergence of a chicken support group.

The underlying conflict was not about chickens. To an extent, it was about being able to do what you want to in your own back yard. More important, it was about simpler times when everybody had chickens. It was also about relationships, both neighbor to neighbor and human to chicken.

Summary

The examples in this section focused on volunteer organizations, neighborhood associations, and community organizations. These types of enterprises provide vivid illustrations of the delusion of having consensus. However, they have by no means cornered the market for this delusion.

Government agencies also frequently experience this delusion. Officially and formally, everybody agrees on goals and strategies. Once you delve below the surface, you find another system. The high-level consensus so common with this delusion plays little role for those who are successful in creating and maintaining government programs. Research has revealed that successes are highly related to use of the bottom-up approach to consensus discussed earlier.

Business organizations also frequently suffer from the consensus delusion. As with other types of organizations, the high-level agreement syndrome is a common basis for it. The bottom-up approach to building real consensus is useful in business environments but less useful than in government because market forces and accountability are so much stronger in business.

The approach that deals directly with needs and beliefs and their role in conflicts is very much applicable and is often invoked when dealing with crises. We have employed this approach when dealing with conflicts involving environmental issues, defense conversion, and quality programs. In all cases, the approach led to new insights and considerable progress.

The delusion of consensus stems from a basic inability to deal with the fact of disagreements. It is so much easier and more comfortable to assume that we are all singing from the same sheet of music. The fact that we are not is both a problem to be resolved and an opportunity to be pursued. We have to stop pretending and start taking advantage of the multiple perspectives often underlying disagreement and conflict.

Central Principles

Exhibit 7.1 summarizes the discussion in this chapter in terms of several conflict principles. The key to avoiding the delusion of consensus is to avoid expecting complete agreement. If apparent consensus is achieved by avoiding underlying disagreements, then consensus becomes a delusion.

Exhibit 7.1. Conflict Principles.

- Expectations of complete agreement can lead to unexpected and substantial disagreements.

- If consensus is achieved by avoiding underlying disagreements, then consensus becomes a delusion.

- Consensus is only an agreement to act, not necessarily agreement on all the actions to be taken.

- Exposing and exploring differences of needs and beliefs can provide a basis for negotiating win-win resolutions of conflicts that would otherwise undermine progress.

- People's needs and beliefs affect what knowledge is gained, what facts are sought, and how both are interpreted.

- Patiently exploring the basis of conflicts can lead to creative win-win solutions.

- When searching for win-win solutions, expand the scope of the discussion to enable trade-offs across more issues.

- Searching for win-win solutions amidst disagreements and differences usually results in much better strategic thinking.

You must recognize and communicate that you are only seeking an agreement to act, not complete agreement on all the actions to be taken. In fact, underlying disagreements can be a rich source of creative solutions.

Exploring these disagreements in terms of differing needs and beliefs can help in negotiating agreements. In this process, it is important to understand how needs and beliefs influence perceptions. Solutions should support needs and not conflict with beliefs, unless needs and beliefs can be constructively changed.

This approach to understanding conflicts can enable identifying win-win solutions in which everyone's needs are met to some extent. A good tactic for finding win-win possibilities is to expand the scope of the discussion to enable trade-offs across more issues. Overall, searching for win-win solutions amidst disagreements and differences can yield important insights and ideas that would not have been identified otherwise.

Many organizations have a keen need for consensus, which often leads to a delusion of consensus that can completely undermine productivity and effectiveness. The key is to recognize disagreements and differences as assets, not liabilities. Of course, as with other types of assets, disagreements and differences must be managed to yield desired returns.

Key Questions

The key to avoiding the delusion of consensus involves first recognizing the true nature of consensus and then understanding how dealing directly with disagreements can lead to much better strategies, plans, and solutions. Exhibit 7.2 lists several questions that can help you do this. These questions reflect the principles just discussed.

The essence of the delusion discussed in this chapter is *not* a matter of whether consensus is important and valuable but the unfortunate consequences you eventually and inevitably face when you proceed on the basis of an apparent consensus that does not exist. You may try to bury disagreements, but they tend to rise again and demand attention—often when you are least prepared to deal with them.

Exhibit 7.2. Managing Conflicts of Values and Priorities.

- Have you ever thought there was a consensus only to later discover there were actually strong disagreements?

- Can your organization agree to take action despite unresolved disagreements about elements of the action plans?

- How often have disagreements in your organization had sources much deeper than the surface features of the disagreements?

- What are the needs and beliefs that underlie any recent or ongoing conflicts in your organization?

- Can you negotiate win-win solutions by scoping the set of issues to ensure that at least some needs are met for all stakeholders?

Accepting and facing disagreements need not prevent you from taking action. You usually can reach a consensus to act despite disagreements on elements of your plans. Taking action can yield information that helps to resolve disagreements. At the same time, paying attention to underlying disagreements can provide insights that enable a creative reformulation of your plans.

We Have to Make the Numbers
Balancing Short Term and Long Term

Strategic planning often begins with discussions of goals. People frequently articulate their goals in terms of sales, profits, market share, and related measures. Such goals might be based on competitive analyses handed down by corporate parents or may simply reflect the burning desires of executives and managers.

Top-level financial goals are usually spread across business units and divisions. Each profit center has its share of the overall goals—its numbers to make. The marketing and sales people try to make the revenue numbers. The people in engineering and manufacturing try to make the cost numbers. Finance people regularly project all the numbers, as well as account for results.

This time-honored process is reasonable, but the rhyme and reason of the process often gets distorted. Short-term numbers tend to dominate tactics and action plans, while long-term numbers receive scant attention. *Making the numbers* means making this quarter's numbers—or this year's numbers.

A short-term focus is natural. Marketing and sales people are compensated for this year's revenues, not next year's. Many people's bonuses depend on staying within this year's budget, not next year's. The stock market often reacts negatively when its expectations for this quarter's or this year's numbers are not met.

The near term is compelling, and it often appears that there are many more options for dealing with the longer term. Hence, people feel that decisions can be delayed until the range of alternatives narrows—until the market or other forces winnow the set of options. The result tends to be a complete focus on short-term issues, for example, this month's payroll rather than next year's sales. Strategic thinking and planning receive little quality attention when new perspectives and options are still possibilities. The delusion of having to make the numbers *now* undermines the possibility of making the numbers later.

I can imagine that some readers are saying to themselves, "What delusion? If I don't make my numbers, I'm gone!" I do not, by any means, doubt this. The delusion I'm talking about is not necessarily yours. It is the company's notion that having people focus only on today's numbers will create long-term success.

The key to avoiding this delusion is to approach short-term and long-term trade-offs in a way that creates a balanced portfolio. In other words, alternative investments (for example, in people or technology) should be linked to potential payoffs in both the short term and the long term. The choices among these alternatives should ensure balance both today and tomorrow.

The first step in creating this balance involves recognizing the overall softness in the numbers you are trying to make. It's highly unlikely that the goals you are feverishly trying to accomplish this year—for instance, a 10 percent increase of sales and a 20 percent increase of profits—are heaven sent. For this example, an 11 percent sales increase and 19 percent profit increase are probably equally desirable.

More important, how do this year's sales and revenues trade off against next year's, or those five years from now? These trade-offs are hard to think about, much less operationalize. Nevertheless, it is certainly imaginable that extreme emphasis on today's profits could undermine the investments necessary for achieving profits five years from now.

In general, how will your actions today affect your organization five years from now? This is a difficult question to answer in terms of sales and profits but is tractable if you move away from numbers and focus on value added in the marketplace. What value do you want to add in what markets by what year?

This question about the future could lead you to consider customers' likely needs and wants, technological trends and possible developments, and potential market channels. You might, for instance, focus on information needs, trends in networking, and how value could be added to information services to enhance usefulness and usability. This type of thinking would also lead to considering potential sales and profits and the investments necessary for making these sales and achieving these profits. And it should lead to defining the milestones that need to be accomplished to meet these long-term goals. Plans should then be formulated for achieving these milestones.

Balancing the short term and the long term involves trading off today's sales and profits against achieving milestones on which future sales and profits depend. This trade-off is usually resolved in favor of today's numbers, in some cases severely compromising the possible achievement of key milestones. Why does this happen?

Three reasons seem most common. First, as noted earlier, today's problems are much, much more compelling than tomorrow's problems. An excellent example of this phenomenon is the almost complete unwillingness on the part of the public and the U.S. Congress to compromise today's Social Security and Medicare benefits to ensure the long-term survival of these federal programs.

Second, longer-term plans are often discounted, partly because future profits are less valuable than current profits due to inflation and to the time value of money, that is, the carrying costs of investments needed now to ensure future returns. The rest of the discount is due to lack of confidence in having correctly anticipated future market opportunities. In other words, people are unsure that their long-term investments in, for example, technology will really pay off in the marketplace.

The third reason is our society's almost complete preoccupation with today's returns. As noted earlier, most reward and incentive systems place total emphasis on current performance. We tend to keep score of everything and hand out rewards and respect on the basis of these scores.

So, people are being reasonable when they feel compelled to make their numbers, but they and their organizations are deluded when they think and act as if short-term numbers are all that matter. Those who create a balance between the short term and the long term will experience substantially more long-term success.

Balancing Short Term and Long Term

Three examples will illustrate the delusion of having to make the numbers. I will show the symptoms of the delusion and the ways organizations tend to deal with it in illustrations drawn from R&D planning in industry consortia, organizational development in companies, and efforts to balance environmental trade-offs in communities.

Providing Returns on Membership

I have worked with several industry consortia in the semiconductor, electronics, computer, and electric power industries. All of these experiences were related to collaborative R&D projects, either particular projects or the planning of an overall portfolio of projects. These planning efforts provided substantial insight into the nature of consortia.

A basic premise of these organizations is that collaborative R&D will help all of the member companies solve common problems. These solutions will be obtained at a small fraction of the cost for each member, compared to the costs if they had proceeded alone. A potential disadvantage of this approach is the resulting broad availability of the solutions created.

The process of reaching agreement on a set of common problems to be addressed provides a view of member companies' priorities. Two forces strongly affect this agenda-setting process. First, member companies do not want competitive technologies on the agenda, unless of course they are at a disadvantage relative to these technologies. Second, members want investments made in areas where they will gain substantial—and, if possible, auditable—returns on their membership fees and costs of participation.

The confluence of these two forces results in many crucial R&D issues being precluded from pursuit, while heavily populating the R&D agenda with issues that produce an easily quantifiable return on investment. Near-term issues are more crisply specified; hence, results in these areas are more easily measured. Long-term issues, in contrast, are usually less crisp, and the value of resolving these issues is subject to many uncertainties.

The predictable result is that consortia, in having to make the numbers for their members, create R&D agendas crowded with relatively short-term priorities. As a result, staff members of consortia have told me that they primarily augment the engineering staffs of the member companies rather than perform R&D. Staff of the member companies have made the same observations.

Thus, the pressure to focus on the short term affects the member companies, both internally with their own R&D staffs and externally as participants in R&D consortia. As a result, R&D becomes just D. The function that was created to focus on the long term falls prey to the delusion of having to make the numbers.

The senior personnel who represent member companies on the boards of directors or advisers of consortia strongly influence this trend. When consortia are first founded, it is common for a top executive—often the CEO—to be a board member. However, as the venture ages, this responsibility is usually passed on to the top executives' lieutenants who, in time, pass it on to their staff members.

Within a few years, this responsibility is carried by a middle manager who faces strong pressures at home to make the numbers and who, as a result, brings this same pressure to bear on the consortium. The original motivation for forming the consortium is thus undermined. The delusion of having to make the numbers—and the consequent short-term focus—results in a scramble for quick, measurable results that is incompatible with the design and staffing of the organization.

Muddling Through

Almost all organizations expect entry-level personnel to arrive educated in business, finance, chemistry, engineering, or some other discipline. The organization then provides context-specific training in the tasks these people will perform in the company, agency, or institution. In this way, general knowledge is transformed to specific skills.

As these people succeed with their initial tasks, they are promoted to other, more important tasks. This process continues until some of them have substantial responsibilities. I have worked with people who have gained responsibility for the overall design of new products or responsibility for developing business strategies.

Several of my projects have focused on the knowledge and skills necessary to succeed with these types of responsibilities. Clearly, individuals' technical skills and knowledge of an organization provide a good starting point. However, they need a variety of additional concepts, principles, methods, and tools if they are to succeed in thinking strategically and developing useful and usable plans.

Beyond gaining this new knowledge and skills, people need coaching to help them transform principles to practice. These soon-to-be product managers and strategic planners need to have role models they can observe and emulate. They need someone who can relate stories of successes—and especially stories of failures.

Few people gain such new knowledge and skills, and few have this type of support. Instead people with new-found responsibilities respond to the pressure to get on with it by muddling through in one way or another. When asked about this situation, one senior manager told me, "I am so busy underperforming, I don't have time to get good at this."

The pressure to make the numbers results in little time to gain the knowledge and skills necessary for performing well. This pressure, combined with frequent intrusions of day-to-day issues, results in muddling through to achieve short-term results while sacrificing the ability to more effectively and efficiently achieve long-term results. Consequently, key competencies in strategic thinking are not created. Muddling through to make today's numbers causes tomorrow's numbers to be no easier to make. In fact, they will be more difficult to make because competitors are often gaining competencies that the organization is, in effect, avoiding. To a great extent, people suffering from this delusion are acting as though there is no tomorrow.

Overcoming the delusion does not require that you turn your back on short-term financial goals. Instead, you can make substantial progress by isolating 5 to 10 percent of your resources (your time, people, and money) and allocating them for the long term. Don't let these resources be preempted by short-term needs. Make sure they are focused on key long-term needs.

This, of course, requires that you identify long-term needs and focus on meeting them, which brings up issues such as visions, goals, strategies, and plans. Resolving these issues requires that you deal with a variety of uncertainties and risks. It requires that you choose a few things to deal with that are strategically critical to your future and avoid dealing with many things that are not.

Many people have difficulty making such choices. As a result, their future has little if any focus. They simply assume that in the future they will be doing pretty much what they are doing now. Their total focus on the present preempts them from defining the future. Their inability to define the future in terms of goals, strategies, and plans makes it impossible for them to focus a portion of their energies on this future.

Thus, having to make the numbers is not only a delusion, it is a trap. Total focus on today's numbers traps you in the present, unable to see a future. Inability to see a future results in the present being your only alternative. You have to break this debilitating spiral if you are to escape the trap and move beyond the delusion.

Having No Choice

The ways in which industry, government, and people in general approach environmental issues provide good illustrations of difficult trade-offs between short-term and long-term concerns. Typically, the debate involves current economic returns, that is, making the numbers now versus long-term consequences and costs. The delusion that often emerges, particularly on the industry side of issues, is that making today's numbers is really all that counts.

A few years ago, I was a member of an advisory committee overseeing the resolution of a major toxic waste disposal problem. The disposal problem emerged when communities near several of the waste storage sites took action to force removal of the toxic waste. The government agency involved had concluded that the waste was best incinerated where it was stored. The communities opposed this plan and wanted the waste removed and destroyed elsewhere. Interestingly, the surrounding communities also blocked efforts to transport the waste through their communities, thereby making it impossible to remove it.

The on-site incineration plan eventually prevailed. The deciding factor was the multi-billion-dollar contract awarded for construction of the "demanufacturing" facilities. Once it became clear how much money and how many jobs were involved, these communities changed their tunes. In fact, I recently learned that one of the communities has mounted a campaign to have more waste moved into their area in order to keep the factory open and not lose the high-paying jobs.

The potential longer-term consequences of having a toxic waste dump and disposal facility in the back yard gave way to the short-term desire to make the numbers—in this case, the local payroll. In retrospect, this is not surprising. We all have to make our numbers each month to pay our mortgage and other bills.

Actually, we *choose* to make our numbers. We are not required to have any particular lifestyle. Similarly, companies are not required to achieve particular sales levels and profitability targets. However, for both individuals and companies, it is much easier to proceed as if you have no choice. This strong tendency is the essence of the delusion.

Some of my customers are producers of toxic wastes as by-products of their manufacturing processes. They are not unusual. All of their competitors produce the same wastes. In one of my client companies, the idea emerged that toxin-free manufacturing could provide a substantial future competitive advantage. It was argued that this ability, in conjunction with the ability to recycle 100 percent of returned products, would provide a tremendous advantage. The company could become the only truly environmentally friendly manufacturer of these types of products.

This idea encountered two primary difficulties, both of which relate to current economic returns. First, naysayers were concerned about the investments necessary to develop the capabilities for toxin-free manufacturing and 100 percent recycling. Second, they cited readily available data indicating that consumers will pay little if any premium for environmentally friendly products.

The proponents countered by emphasizing their intentions to develop these abilities in ways that did not raise prices to consumers. More important, they said, were regulatory trends, especially in Europe, that will eventually result in toxin-free manufacturing being a requirement. Thus, they argued, the investments they were proposing would have to be made eventually. Why not make them when they provided a competitive advantage?

In the end, the proposal was trapped by the near-term financial implications. The company had a very difficult time sacrificing the current numbers for the prospects of more attractive but uncertain future numbers. If they had chosen to make this sacrifice, they might have proceeded with vigor. However, they were caught in a delusion that they could not willingly make the sacrifice.

Summary

The three examples discussed in this section illustrate the strong tendencies and substantial consequences of the delusion of having to make the numbers. I could relate many other experiences with companies and other types of enterprises whose thinking is totally dominated by the present. This delusion is as common as pigeons in New York City's Central Park.

This is not surprising. The present can be very compelling, whereas the future is inherently uncertain. It is, therefore, natural to focus on the short term and somehow muddle through. However, strategic advantage seldom emerges from such behavior.

The key, as in many things, is balance. Making the short-term numbers provides the means for achieving longer-term goals. Paying sufficient attention to these long-term goals provides the means for defining the futurity of short-term behavior. Without this linkage and balance, you can easily become trapped in the vicious circle of only dealing with the short term because you are unable to define the long term.

Central Principles

Exhibit 8.1 summarizes the lessons learned in this chapter in terms of several balance principles. The delusion of having to make the numbers involves complete focus on this quarter's or this year's numbers, which results in little if any attention being paid to future numbers and, consequently, little investment being made in future returns.

A short-term focus also tends to preempt gaining the knowledge and skills necessary for dealing successfully with long-term

---

Exhibit 8.1. Balance Principles.

- Making the numbers often means making this quarter's numbers or, at most, this year's numbers.

- The delusion of having to make the numbers now often undermines the possibility of making the numbers later.

- Extreme emphasis on today's profits undermines investments necessary for achieving future profits.

- The pressure to make the numbers results in little time to gain the knowledge and skills necessary to performing well.

- Strategic thinking and planning often receive little quality attention while new options are still possible.

- Total focus on today's numbers traps you in the present, unable to see a future. The inability to see a future results in the present being your only alternative

- Explicitly decide on an appropriate balance between short-term and long-term goals for your organization.

- Choose those few things that are strategically critical to your future. Avoid the many things that are not.

- We all choose to make our numbers; however, the natural tendency is to proceed as if there is no choice.

---

issues. People either avoid strategic thinking and planning, or they muddle through. Without a cogent long-term view, people are trapped in the present.

To avoid this delusion and its debilitating consequences, you should decide on an appropriate balance between short-term and long-term goals for your organization. In considering long-term goals, choose those few things that are strategically critical to your future. Avoid the many things that are not.

Your ability and motivation to create the necessary balance will be enhanced if you recognize a simple truth. You choose to make your numbers. The natural tendency is to proceed as if you have no choice. The delusion emerges from the failure to recognize this choice.

Key Questions

The key to avoiding the delusion of having to make the numbers involves first recognizing the substantial perils of this trap and then intentionally allocating at least a modest portion of your energies to the future. Exhibit 8.2 lists several questions that can help you do this. The questions reflect the principles just discussed.

The essence of the delusion discussed in this chapter is *not* a matter of the importance of short-term numbers. They are important. Short-term goals inherently require most of your attention. The problem is in the debilitating consequences of focusing only on the short term. To avoid this trap, you need focused long-term goals and investments linked to these goals.

Making the numbers becomes a delusion when you forget that you have strategic choices to make. Short-term issues and needs will inevitably take much of your time. If you let them dominate, however, you will become trapped. To avoid this dilemma, you have to create a balance between short term and long term. You have to create this balance and manage your time so that balance is maintained.

Exhibit 8.2. Balancing Short Term and Long Term.

- Have your short-term focus and your lack of long-term goals resulted in your being trapped in the present with little if any view of the future?

- What recent instances are indicative of your organization's abilities to sacrifice short-term returns for potential long-term gains?

- What investments are you making whose primary returns will be in the long term?

- What knowledge and skills are you gaining that will provide competencies for dealing with the long term?

- Is your long-term thinking focused on the few critical things that matter? Are you vigilantly avoiding the many possible diversions?

Part Three

Make Sure That Plans Lead to Actions

We Have the Ducks Lined Up
Navigating the Tangled Webs of Relationships

Before developing new strategies and plans, it is useful to review the results of past strategies and plans. During such reviews, people often say they thought their plans were pretty good but somehow did not lead to the desired results. This leads to the obvious question, Why?

The most frequent answer is that they ran into unexpected problems in implementation. A typical difficulty involves discovering that there are more stakeholders than expected. Another relates to having an inadequate infrastructure—perhaps even one that is a burden on the hoped-for implementation.

Without doubt, the most significant implementation problem is poor or inadequate execution. Plans that may be carefully formulated and show great potential nevertheless end up shelved. Implementation starts, but key people get distracted. Fire fighting preempts tree planting. Slower-than-expected results lead to loss of enthusiasm and consequently to a lack of attention to continued implementation.

This chapter and the next two chapters focus on an essential element of successful strategic thinking—making sure that plans lead to actions. Delusions that plans can be easily implemented—and, in fact, are being implemented—lead to poor performance or a complete lack of performance. The key to avoiding these types of delusions is to have plans for implementing your plans.

This chapter deals with the delusion of already having your ducks lined up for implementation when, in fact, you have failed to deal with relationships that are essential to success. Subsequent chapters focus on the delusion that your existing infrastructure will fully support plan implementation, as well as the delusion that committed execution is under way.

Relationships are usually central to success. It is impossible to be a business success without having relationships with customers. Typically, there are also relationships with users, salespeople, distributors, suppliers, employees, stockholders, and so on. Success often involves understanding and managing the tangled web of relationships among these and other stakeholders in your economic food chain.

The intermediate stakeholders in these food chains—or value chains—often have needs and desires that go beyond providing end customers with quality products and services. Salespeople want products that are easy to explain and that provide compelling value. Distributors want high volumes and discounts. Employees want stable and rewarding jobs. Stockholders want competitive returns on their investments.

The web of relationships underlying your potential success can become very complicated, as later vignettes illustrate. Diagnosing relationship problems in your value chain requires understanding what roles different stakeholders play, what rewards they seek, and what commitments they will make. This knowledge should help you ensure that all the stakeholders in your goals and plans are supported and supportive.

I find that the best way to do this is to list all of your stakeholders, as well as their concerns, values, and perceptions. It is also valuable to identify measures of the extent to which stakeholders' needs are supported. You then can assess both your offerings and those of your competitors. I discuss methods and tools for this type of analysis in *Best Laid Plans* (Rouse, 1994).

This type of analysis provides the basis for implementing a very powerful strategy. Put simply, success is guaranteed if you delight your primary stakeholders and gain the support of your secondary stakeholders. The key, then, is to determine how to provide delights and how to gain support.

Navigating Tangled Webs of Relationships

The first step toward solving any navigation problem is usually to obtain or create a map. This is also true for navigating relationships among stakeholders in your plans. Creating a relationship map requires that you identify all the types of stakeholders who are likely to affect your success and then determine their concerns, values, and perceptions in the context of your intentions. In this section, I discuss three illustrations of this process.

Having It Made

We tend to think of Boeing as the largest manufacturer of commercial aircraft. However, this company is in fact the largest *assembler* of commercial aircraft, most components of which are manufactured by other companies. Boeing is a systems developer and integrator, and as such is responsible for planning how all the components will come together and then ensuring that they do. The result should be an efficient and safe aircraft that meets the needs of the airlines.

Let's say that you have a great idea for helping aircraft pilots fly more efficiently and safely. Perhaps you have researched this idea, developed the concept, and evaluated its impact with pilots in flight simulators. You are now ready, you think, to have your idea incorporated into the design of commercial aircraft. What's the next step?

It seems obvious that you should contact Boeing and try to convince them to include this idea in the design of their next cockpit. When you knock on Boeing's door, however, you find that the situation is much more complicated than you expected. Boeing isn't interested unless a major airline, say Delta Air Lines, has asked for what you are proposing. Further, because Boeing mainly assembles things built by others, they aren't interested unless a major avionics company, say Honeywell, is willing and able to design and develop your innovation.

You now see that you must convince at least three classes of stakeholders: the aircraft manufacturer, the airlines, and the avionics companies. However, you soon discover that there are more than three. The Federal Aviation Administration has to certify the safety of your finished product, as well as the process whereby it is produced. End users—pilots and perhaps air traffic controllers—also must be considered.

The complexity of this network of relationships is not unique to the aviation industry. Consider the power industry in general and the nuclear power industry in particular. This industry also has many players, including consumers, utilities, contractors, the Nuclear Regulatory Commission, and a variety of groups that are either for or against nuclear power.

The stakeholders in this world often have diametrically opposed priorities and preferences. Keeping track of this network of relationships and positioning your ideas can be very difficult. My experience in this industry is that potential innovations tend to get little attention because of the many regulatory issues demanding attention.

When my previous company was heavily involved in this industry, I asked a senior executive how best to articulate the benefits of a particular idea. He suggested that benefits and costs were irrelevant. My only hope was to get the idea to be a regulatory requirement. Otherwise, I would never get a serious hearing.

In the end, we changed our strategy, shifted our energies elsewhere, and phased out our business in this industry. A conservative, declining industry that is avoiding innovation if at all possible is not the best place to try to sell new ideas. Further, the cost of maintaining the relationship network was too high. The companies that stayed in the industry were mainly those whose costs of exit were too great.

The situations depicted here for the aviation and power industries involve many kinds of people or stakeholders, most of whom have differing preferences and priorities. You have to position your products or services amidst this web of players and issues. You have to figure out some way to delight—or at least gain the support of—these many types of stakeholders.

The situation is further complicated by changing players and roles. People retire or resign; they are reassigned or promoted. New issues emerge, and old issues fade in importance. You have to keep track of these changes and modify your story accordingly. You have to teach new players how to articulate your story.

The most common delusion in this situation is one of finally having the ducks lined up—finally knowing all the players and their concerns, and finally having convinced all these players of the merits of your offerings. The problem is that staying lined up is not a natural tendency of ducks. Therefore, rather than being relieved that you have the ducks lined up, you must focus on keeping them that way.

Put simply, the way to avoid this delusion is to vigilantly manage the relationship network that is central to your success. You have to keep track of stakeholders and their current priority issues. You have to adapt continually as players and their priorities change. There is no having it made. There is only keeping it made. The key is to avoid the delusion that you have succeeded. You must manage the many relationships and constantly coax and cajole the ducks to keep some semblance of order.

Not Doing Homework

The semiconductor and electronics industries present a somewhat different set of relationship issues. You still have customers, but end users are much less accessible than, for example, aircraft pilots. The thousands, or perhaps millions, of people who use your chips or circuit boards in their personal computers or engine management systems, for instance, are far removed from the process of designing and developing your semiconductors or electronics.

Your relationship network includes original equipment manufacturers, distributors, perhaps retail stores, end users, and maintenance people. You have to infer the concerns, values, and perceptions of all the players in this food chain. Unlike the aviation and power industries, you cannot get all the players together and work through design decisions.

It is difficult to line up ducks you can't see. To avoid this limitation, companies in these industries often perform market research focused on their customers' customers. They try to second guess their customers' future priorities by assessing the likely demands of downstream customers.

It is especially hard to assess the future use of end products. For example, can you reasonably assume that most computer users three years from now will have CD-ROM drives on their computers?

If this assumption is reasonable, you can—and should—include a variety of multimedia functions and features on the new software product you are planning. If CD-ROMs are unlikely to be common for the next three to five years, however, you should not invest heavily in multimedia options that most users will not value.

The delusion of having the ducks lined up usually emerges in the process of identifying the stakeholders in the relationship networks in these industries and determining their concerns, values, and perceptions. People in these high-tech industries—especially technology people—tend to assume that they understand their markets thoroughly. This assumption usually remains untested until they suddenly discover ducks out of line, or perhaps even new ducks.

Even though the delusion persists, poor investment decisions often prevail. A common mistake is to invest in more technology than the market can absorb. People create the fastest, smallest, or lightest widget based on the erroneous and unspoken assumption that their markets are waiting with bated breath for the extreme versions of widgets. But they may find that their markets cannot take advantage of more speed, for example, because of constraints imposed by other technologies.

The underlying problem is not inadequate market research. Often, it is a complete lack of market research. Usually, appropriate analyses of market data are lacking as well. People simply assume that they know their markets in general, and the key players and their needs and desires in particular—an assumption that results in the delusion of having the ducks lined up.

Avoiding this delusion involves doing your homework. It means identifying stakeholders and talking with them. It means researching market and technology trends. Finally, it means analyzing and determining how the different pieces of the puzzle fit together. Unfortunately, these types of activities are often preempted by the strong push to get on with it.

It is natural to want to get on with using your competencies to create the products and services you feel—or think you know—your markets want. It takes discipline to delay acting until you are sure of your assumptions. This need not mean long delays. Often, a few weeks are ample to clarify the relationship network, roles of players in the network, and their relevant needs and wants.

As reasonable as these activities sound, they are often avoided. People seem to think that getting good information will take too long, so they proceed with little or no information. Rather than spend $50,000 to make sure they understand key relationship networks and their implications, they spend $100,000,000 to create a product or service that is a market failure. The benefit to such decision makers, of course, is that they were able to get on with it.

Just a Few Good Ducks

Relationship networks in large volunteer organizations can also be complex. Key stakeholder groups include volunteers, paid staff members, contributors, and beneficiaries. The general public can also be an important constituency.

Within these species of ducks are many variations. Volunteers are often deeply invested in a single issue rather than the organization's broad agenda. Contributors can also be focused. The confluence of this wide variety of foci can result in staff members being pulled in many directions, often unable to focus on the goals and plans for which they are responsible.

Trying to line up the ducks in such organizations is further complicated by differences among national, regional, and local perspectives. There are inevitable tensions between "the field" where services are provided, congregations meet, and so forth, and regional or national efforts to orchestrate the bigger picture. Miniversions of the states' rights versus federalist debate happen again and again.

This type of environment requires a very different approach to lining up ducks. It is virtually impossible to get broad agreement, or even a consensus to act, prior to proceeding with an idea. I recently asked executives of one of the largest volunteer organizations in the United States what strategy works best when trying to get new ideas going. They suggested that I avoid getting all the ducks lined up. They said, in effect, "Just get a few ducks lined up. If you can then show tangible success, other ducks will slowly but surely align themselves."

The important difference between the volunteer organizations and the earlier examples of the aviation, power, semiconductor, and electronics industries is the nature of the governing rationale.

In private sector industries, technical and economic perspectives tend to dominate discourse and decision making. In contrast, volunteer organizations are much more influenced by social and political perspectives.

The consequence of this difference is that you seldom can get everybody aligned in volunteer organizations. Relatively few of the stakeholders are being paid to be involved, so the top-down decision making that usually works in private sector industries is rarely an alternative. Instead, you have to coax and cajole a few ducks at a time to support your idea or proposal. Once you get a critical mass of ducks lined up, you simply act.

Summary

The three examples discussed in this section are very different. The example from the aviation and power industries illustrates complicated networks of relationships. However, the stakeholders in these industries are well defined and accessible. Thus, you can know the concerns of all stakeholders and, in fact, interact with all stakeholders.

The example from the semiconductor and electronics industries also illustrates complicated relationship networks. The stakeholders in these industries are reasonably well defined, but many are not readily accessible. As a result, you have to infer their concerns. This creates increased chances for error in your perceptions of the alignment of the ducks.

Large volunteer organizations tend to be sufficiently complicated to prevent lining up ducks at all. Substantial heterogeneity across the agendas of the many stakeholders renders broadly based consensus almost impossible in the absence of compelling success stories. The result is that relatively narrow coalitions often proceed without broader support, in an effort to create success before attempting to line up such support.

Despite these differences, the key to navigating tangled webs of relationships remains the same: make sure you understand your stakeholders and their concerns, values, and perceptions. In some cases, this will enable you to deal with these people and issues directly. In other cases, your understanding will support making inferences regarding people and issues. In yet other cases, this understanding will help you determine which people and issues to avoid. Overall, this understanding will ensure that you avoid the delusion of having the ducks lined up.

Central Principles

Exhibit 9.1 summarizes the lessons learned in this chapter in terms of several relationship principles. The delusion of having the ducks lined up usually stems from a lack of knowledge. It can also arise when you once had the necessary knowledge but have not kept up to date.

The key to avoiding this delusion is to understand and manage relationships with your stakeholders. This requires knowing what roles each of them plays, what stakes they hold, and what types of commitments they might be willing to make. You can capture this knowledge in a relationship map that portrays the concerns, values, and perceptions of stakeholders.

Exhibit 9.1. Relationship Principles.

- The delusion of having the ducks lined up usually stems from not knowing your stakeholders and not understanding their issues.
- Success usually involves understanding and managing the tangled web of relationships among your stakeholders.
- Diagnosing relationship problems requires understanding what roles different stakeholders play, what rewards they seek, and what commitments they will make.
- Creation of a relationship map involves identifying your stakeholders and determining their concerns, values, and perceptions in the context of your intentions.
- Success is guaranteed if you delight your primary stakeholders and gain the support of your secondary stakeholders.
- Staying lined up is not a natural tendency of ducks. You have to focus on keeping them aligned.
- There is no having it made. There is only keeping it made.

This knowledge should enable you to implement a strategy that almost always guarantees success—a strategy involving partitioning your stakeholders into two sets: primary and secondary. You should do everything possible to ensure that your ideas *and* their implementation will delight the primary stakeholders. For the others, you should focus on gaining their support. Delighting them may not be relevant because their stake is only secondary.

Successful execution of this strategy depends on recognizing the fundamental fact that ducks tend to stray outside of lines. You have to keep them in line by paying attention to relationships and making sure your knowledge of concerns, values, and perceptions is up to date. As you get better at executing in this way, you should take care to avoid the feeling that you have it made, which is usually the first symptom of the delusion.

Key Questions

The key to avoiding the delusion of having the ducks lined up is to pay careful attention to identifying your stakeholders and assuring that their concerns, values, and perceptions are considered and balanced. Exhibit 9.2 lists several questions to help you do this. The questions reflect the principles discussed in the last section.

Exhibit 9.2. Navigating Tangled Webs of Relationships.

- Who are the stakeholders that influence the success or failure of your products and services?
- What roles do these stakeholders play, and what is the nature of their stakes?
- Which stakeholders are primary, and which are secondary?
- What benefits of your offerings most delight your primary stakeholders?
- What aspects of your offerings are crucial to gaining the support of secondary stakeholders?

The essence of the delusion discussed in this chapter is *not* a matter of whether it is important to line up the ducks but the consequences of thinking the ducks are aligned when they are not. Avoiding this delusion involves focusing on duck alignment and continuing to do so.

Understanding and managing relationships is key in strategic thinking. There are systematic ways to gain this understanding, as well as methods for supporting the management process—methods that not only increase the effectiveness and efficiency of your strategic thinking but also ensure that this debilitating delusion does not undermine your intentions.

We Have the Necessary Processes
Avoiding Institutionalized Conflicts

How will your new goals, strategies, and plans affect your existing organizational processes? Many executives and senior managers assume that they can play new games with old organizations. They usually hope to find ways to meld existing processes into their intended new directions, often because the prospect of having to rethink organizational processes is so daunting.

By processes, I mean the structures and activities that support finance and accounting, human resources and organizational development, product design and development, manufacturing and assembly, marketing, sales, service, and so on. Put simply, in contrast to the things you do, processes are the ways you do things.

One of the most pervasive, yet sometimes subtle, processes in an organization is the incentive and reward system. Failing to modify this system can substantially undermine an organization's new directions. People will continue to respond to old incentives and rewards despite the system's inconsistency with the organization's stated goals.

For example, a system that emphasizes individual accomplishment will inevitably thwart new organizational emphases on teamwork. Similarly, a system that only keeps score of short-term results will undermine efforts to promote long-term thinking. Few would disagree with these observations, yet many organizations labor under such inconsistencies.

Another example relates to organizational structures. Collaboration among organizational components can be undermined by structures that foster competition for scarce resources. Whereas a mutual husbanding of such resources may be the goal, structures that prompt competition can result in a squirreling away of resources that would otherwise be used productively.

Moving beyond the delusion of having the necessary processes requires a willingness to reconsider your processes in light of new goals, strategies, and plans. You need to think about these new intentions and ask, for example, how your hiring practices, incentive and reward system, and finance and accounting system support these intentions.

You have to design your organization for it to be effective in pursuit of new directions. The organization's natural tendency will be to do things as they have been done in the past. If you want it to be different, you have to redesign it. Otherwise, the delusion that you have the necessary processes is quite likely to render your new directions unachievable.

Without redesign, you will have decided, implicitly at least, to support institutionalized conflict. You will have put in play a game that cannot be won. Everyone will go through the motions. It may even seem that progress is being made and that evolution will lead to the needed adaptations. However, organisms can rarely evolve fast enough to deal with crises at their door.

Redesign is not just reorganization. It is not merely putting the same sets of activities in different boxes. Redesign involves rethinking work activities in terms of which activities are now appropriate and how tasks should be accomplished. Redesign also involves rethinking incentives and rewards to ensure that they support the transition to the redesigned work activities.

Redesign is, admittedly, a difficult task. It is not a quick fix. Perceptions that redesign will be easy are sure signs of the delusion of having the necessary processes. Such perceptions usually lead to a hopeful muddling through that almost always leads to disappointing results.

One of the most difficult aspects of redesign is implementation. You usually encounter conflict between maintaining the present and creating the future. Often, present activities are providing the cash flow to enable future activities, so you cannot simply stop doing one thing and start doing another.

The best way to deal with this conflict is to consider the transition from present to future to be another design task. Rather than defining the future and then just crossing your fingers, you need to design how present activities transition into future activities. The goal is to create a map that shows people how and when their current work activities will transition into their future jobs. This map can help substantially, but it does not eliminate work. It doesn't change the fact that reaching the goal of being a mountain climber requires climbing. But even though hard work must be done, at least everyone will know what work to do and how to do it.

Avoiding Institutionalized Conflicts

Three examples illustrate the nature of the delusion of having the necessary processes, including the ways this delusion affects organizations' abilities to change and innovate. Understanding the substantial impact of your processes is the first step to avoiding this delusion.

Playing by the Rules

We tend to think of universities as being hotbeds of innovation—bellwethers of new trends in art, science, technology, and lifestyles. This is true for the *products* of the universities—their research, publications, and especially students. However, it is far from true for their *processes*.

Many university processes reflect traditions that started in Europe in the Middle Ages and have been nurtured over the intervening centuries. A few administrative processes are as new as World War II. The federal government's annual investments of billions of dollars in university research have certainly shaped the ways universities do business.

Creating innovative products in the context of conservative, often antiquated, processes presents a variety of dilemmas. Perhaps the best example is the promotion and tenure process in universities. I successfully made it through this process in the late 1970s and since then have served as an outside reviewer for many tenure and promotion cases for a wide variety of universities.

Incentives and rewards in academia are almost totally linked to individual accomplishments, especially to faculty members' abilities to publish books and articles and to obtain grant monies. To get full credit for these accomplishments, you have to work alone. You can supervise the work of graduate student members of your research team, but you should avoid collaborating with other faculty members. Such collaboration tends to result in having to split the credit for accomplishments.

Put simply, to get promoted and become tenured, you need to formulate enough theories, collect enough data, or prove enough theorems to publish three to five research articles per year. At the same time, you need to write winning grant proposals that will secure the dollars to do this research.

The rules are very clear. So are the results. Faculty members focus on efforts that can be accomplished by one person (with student helpers) and yield publications at the necessary rate. After four to six years of doing this, your chances of getting promoted and being granted tenure are good.

The consequence of this process is that most faculty members, especially junior faculty members, focus on very small problems. Participating in multidisciplinary teams addressing complex multidimensional problems is a sure way to get a pink slip. As a result, the institution of which we expect the most innovation can only innovate "in the small."

Universities' delusion that they have the necessary processes makes it almost impossible for them to tackle big problems. This is not just due to their antiquated incentive and reward system but to processes that have institutionalized interorganization conflict.

An excellent example concerns the distribution of overhead monies. Major research universities receive enormous amounts of reimbursed overhead from the federal government. This overhead is loosely associated with the costs of conducting research that is supported by federal grants and contracts. Included in overhead are the costs of facilities, computers, libraries, and so forth.

Most universities distribute a portion of the reimbursed overhead to the organizations that generated these monies by winning contracts and grants. This immediately raises the question of who gets the credit for each contract and grant. My own experience is that the process of attributing credit and securing pieces of the overhead pie can lead to substantial conflicts.

Multidisciplinary research centers especially can be plagued by such conflicts. These centers—or laboratories or institutes—involve faculty members from multiple academic departments. These "home" departments expect their faculty members to generate overhead funds, which the departments can apply to a variety of needs. However, the centers also need these funds to provide seed corn for new efforts, as well as to cover indirect costs.

Faculty members become torn between their allegiances to centers and to home departments. One such faculty member told me that an appointment of 50 percent time in a center and 50 percent time in an academic department always ends up with 75 percent in each, trying to keep everybody happy. You would think that such conflicts would cause universities to reconsider their processes, but they are trapped by the delusion of having the necessary processes.

One of the universities where I spent many years had a committee on committees. The purpose of this committee was to ensure that committee memberships were representative of the university community. More simply, its purpose was to make certain that everyone had a share of the power and resources available. The result was a highly politicized system in which it was impossible to make anything other than small, incremental changes. Thus, the university had created a mechanism that sustained the delusion of having the necessary processes.

In light of the dysfunctional nature of many processes in universities, it would seem that redesign is needed. However, as many former university presidents can attest, redesign in universities is all but impossible. It is not like redesigning a business. It is more like redesigning a religion.

Faculty members who are paragons of rationality within their academic disciplines are seldom as rational when discussing how the university should be managed. When coherent arguments against change are lacking, they can always rely on the rallying cry of academic freedom. Tradition becomes a heavy anchor. So, innovation in universities is often led by people who work around the system. They accomplish things in spite of any processes that are in their way. For example, they pursue complex research problems and assemble multidisciplinary teams despite the risks and lack of rewards. Innovation does happen. Much more could happen if universities could overcome the delusion of having the necessary processes.

Precluding Trade-Offs

Government organizations can provide a wealth of illustrations of this delusion, partly because they are "process rich," with a wide variety of processes being legally mandated for almost every aspect of their operations. Frequently, these processes thwart all efforts to achieve important goals.

An excellent example drawn from the Department of Defense concerns the problem of supporting the operators and maintainers of complex weapon systems. Specifically, the issue of interest involves a fundamental trade-off between investing in the technology underlying weapon systems and investing in the personnel who operate and maintain these systems.

This trade-off concerns finding a balance between two extremes. On the one hand, the DOD might invest in sufficient technology (for example, automation technology and "smart" diagnostic systems) to make it possible to use operators and maintainers with minimal training. On the other hand, the DOD might invest in sophisticated training that produces operators and maintainers who can handle almost anything.

Neither of these extremes is feasible. Technology can be very expensive and cannot do everything. Training can only be as sophisticated as the aptitudes of people who volunteer for the military. The question, then, is how to find the balance between these extremes.

As obvious as this trade-off is, it seldom is addressed in the DOD, where processes preclude substantive approaches to the issue. The acquisition of weapon systems is functionally separate from the design and delivery of training. Even if acquisition and training people interact, neither have the authority or discretionary budgets necessary to make trade-offs across their functional boundaries.

Recognition of this dilemma led me to talk to higher-level DOD executives who have purview of both functional areas. One senior military officer summed up the situation succinctly by noting, "At the level that people have the authority to address this trade-off, they do not understand the nature of the trade-off. At the level that people understand, they do not have the authority."

One consequence is that weapon systems are developed that present significant training challenges. Another is that systems include features that seldom if ever get used. Organizational barriers, as well as incentive and reward systems, preclude modest increases of acquisition costs now to ensure substantially lower training costs later. With few exceptions, this trade-off is never addressed.

Despite a plethora of processes, government agencies frequently undermine their own best interests. The nature of the processes often prompts the following of rules—for example, cost accounting rules—rather than focusing on accomplishing valuable goals. This is at least partially due to the difficulty of assessing the value of many government activities. For example, what is a new research finding worth?

Yet many people in government do achieve innovative and valuable accomplishments. I interviewed several senior DOD executives in Washington, D.C. and asked them how they would explain such successes. The unanimous answer was that the innovators went around the system and short-circuited any processes in their way. They further said that such people tended to be driven by the intrinsic reward of accomplishment rather than the meager extrinsic rewards possible within the government system.

Thus, as with universities, we see people avoiding the delusion of having the necessary processes by circumventing processes. This is a useful tactic in organizations where change is difficult. Such tactics should not be necessary in business organizations where redesign is more common.

Finally Having It Right

Universities and government agencies often re-label their functions and activities and say they have reorganized. Businesses, in contrast, have instituted massive reorganizations in recent years. The result has been delayering, downsizing, rightsizing, and in general trying to do more with less. Much of this activity falls under the rubric of business process reengineering. Leaner or outsourced processes have usually been the outcome. This has contributed substantially to cutting the costs of products and services, and the result has been strong growth of the bottom line.

Many companies are now realizing that they cannot further improve the bottom line (profits) without focusing on increasing the top line (sales). This is resulting in much attention being paid to new products and services, as well as to new markets. It is also resulting in many mergers and acquisitions, as smaller players attempt to become bigger players, and the bigger players try to sustain impressive growth rates.

As these reengineered companies focus on doing new things, they risk succumbing to the delusion that they have the necessary processes. The risk is due to having invested substantially in reengineering and now thinking they have finally got it right. However, what's right for the old business is not necessarily right for the new business.

Success in moving into new markets requires adopting processes that match these markets. As numerous defense companies have repeatedly shown, carrying unnecessary organizational baggage from one industry to another tends to substantially reduce the chances of success. Raytheon's success in transitioning microwave cooking technology to commercial markets was due to their transitioning the technology to Caloric without Raytheon's defense industry processes.

Thus, processes should match markets and even influence the types of new markets that a company pursues. Circuit City's move from retail electronics to selling used automobiles at Carmax is a good illustration of this principle. Circuit City's processes for retail sales, especially the financing of big ticket purchases, provided a strong basis for a whole new approach to used car sales. The two markets are different, but the processes are similar.

Strategic decisions such as Circuit City's should be based on a strong understanding of your processes and the ways in which these processes provide competitive advantages in your markets. If your processes do not provide advantages in the new markets you are entertaining, you should avoid bringing these processes to your new endeavors. Alternatively, as with Circuit City, you can look for new markets where your current processes will provide future advantages. In either case, your processes require strong scrutiny if you are to avoid the delusion of having the necessary processes.

Summary

For plans to lead to actions—and actions to lead to success—you need to have the necessary processes. Otherwise, success only comes when people work outside the system. In universities and government agencies where significant organizational change is immensely difficult, the best strategy may be to help innovators circumvent institutional processes. In business, it is possible to make real changes.

The past decade has seen substantial changes in industry. Many companies have reengineered their processes to dramatically reduce their costs. However, real growth in value is not created by simply paring costs to the bone. Companies have to find new ways to generate revenue so that more can fall through to the bottom line.

As companies scour the landscape for growth opportunities, they risk assuming that they have the necessary processes and now need only add new products and services, in many cases for new markets. This assumption will be a delusion. They need to revisit their processes with each new direction they take, making sure they have not institutionalized conflicts between where they are headed and how they hope to get there.

Central Principles

Exhibit 10.1 lists several process principles gleaned from the lessons learned in this chapter. The delusion of having the necessary processes usually results from a lack of attention, which results in organizations following their natural tendencies to sustain the status quo. Overcoming this tendency requires making a conscious effort to redesign the organization.

Incentive and reward systems can be particularly problematic. Extrinsic systems have to be modified to support new directions. Intrinsic systems also need attention, especially to avoid conflicts with changes of extrinsic systems. Lack of attention to incentives and rewards can easily thwart progress.

Institutionalized conflict among organizational components can undermine efforts to increase collaboration. You need to create win-win situations so that scarce resources are husbanded and targeted to the greatest overall advantage. Otherwise, unrecognized competition may limit the collaboration needed for success.

Exhibit 10.1. Process Principles.

- Organizations' natural tendencies are to do things as they were done in the past. If you want it to be different, you have to redesign it.
- Inability or unwillingness to modify your incentive and reward system can substantially undermine new directions.
- Collaboration among organizational components can be undermined by structures that foster competition for scarce resources.
- Redesign involves rethinking work activities in terms of which activities are now appropriate and how they should be accomplished.
- Perceptions that redesign will be easy are sure signs of the delusion of having the right processes.
- One of the most difficult aspects of redesign is implementation. You usually encounter conflict between maintaining the present while also creating the future.
- Carefully select those elements of the infrastructure of your old organization to cross over to your new organization.
- Rather than defining the future and then just crossing your fingers, you need to design how present activities transition into future activities.

Redesign of your organization involves more than moving boxes around and changing labels. Redesign involves carefully rethinking work activities in terms of their relationships to goals, strategies, and plans. Usually, several significant activities are eliminated and others are added. If you find that little change is needed, it is a sure sign of the delusion of having the necessary processes.

This delusion is particularly plaguing when you attempt to cross over from one market to another. You need to carefully select processes that provide competitive advantage in the new markets. Similarly, you should discard the baggage of processes that provide no advantages. Less is almost always better when making such changes.

Implementation problems are common with redesign. The key is to balance the transition from the present to the future. Achieving this balance involves carefully designing the ways in which present activities transition into future activities.

Key Questions

Put simply, paying attention to processes is the best way to avoid the delusion of having the necessary processes. Exhibit 10.2 lists several questions to help you do this. The questions are based on the principles just discussed.

The essence of the delusion discussed in this chapter is *not* related to the inevitable need for new processes. Many processes that worked in the past will work well in the future. The delusion stems from the unexamined, and usually unrecognized, assumption that the status quo provides a good match for new intentions.

Paying careful attention to process issues is the central concern. If your incentives and rewards are aligned with where you are headed, and structural relationships do not create debilitating barriers, the delusion can likely be avoided. If you have also reviewed other processes to ensure that they match your intentions, you will escape the delusion that you have the necessary processes.

Exhibit 10.2. Avoiding Institutionalized Conflicts.

- Are your organizational processes aligned with your goals, strategies, and plans—or are they in the way?
- Do your incentive and reward systems support execution of your strategy?
- Do the structural relationships among organizational components support your strategy?
- How much of your most recent reorganization was simply the changing of labels?
- How much organizational baggage was eliminated in your most recent reorganization?
- Do you have a transition plan for transforming your old organization and processes into the new?

We Just Have to Execute
Maintaining Commitment and Action

Creating plans is often easier than executing plans. In fact, reluctance to invest in planning is often due to skepticism about whether the resulting plans will be executed. All types of enterprises find it hard to maintain commitment and action.

When people say, "We just have to execute," they often do not understand what "just" means in this context. Their delusion is that when they have finished planning, the difficult work is done. However, sustained and committed execution can be very difficult to achieve.

Many seemingly wonderful plans fail because of execution problems. In some cases, it is due to lackluster execution. In others, it is a complete lack of execution. People tend to say, "We just didn't get around to it."

Why does this happen? A common reason is that neither people nor the financial resources necessary for execution were available. Another is that priorities, either individual or organizational, were inappropriate. The result is that plan execution never makes it to the front of the queue.

Lack of individual and organizational commitment can also be the culprit. Occasionally, in moments of complete honesty, people have told me, "We know that we should be executing the plan, but nobody is really that interested in doing the things the plan requires." Without a champion—someone committed to a plan's success—plans almost always wither on the vine.

One of my mother's favorite sayings is, "The road to Hell is paved with good intentions." This bit of Yankee wisdom captures the essence of the numerous planning purgatories I encounter. Great plans are backed by good intentions but lack any execution.

The underlying problem is that people are easily distracted and usually over-committed to short-term goals and plans. The typical result is that they sit back at the end of each day and say, "What happened?" The days, weeks, and months fly by, and they simply never get around to executing long-term plans.

Thus, execution problems are ubiquitous and are completely natural phenomena. The question is how to overcome them. The answer is to focus on the executability of plans.

Ensuring that plans can be executed involves answering the following questions for each element of your plan:

- Who is going to perform the necessary tasks, and do they have the time to do it?
- How are they going to perform these tasks, and is it reasonable to assume that they can do them?
- What human, physical, and financial resources are needed to perform these tasks, and are these resources available?
- When are these tasks to be completed, and is it reasonable to assume that these targets can be achieved?
- Why will people be committed to performing these tasks, and can anything be done to foster greater commitment?

Answering these questions will ensure that you do not succumb to the delusion of just having to execute.

The questions are fairly elementary; the same guidance can be found in a number of books on project management. Yet the issues raised are frequently ignored. All too often, the unspoken assumption is, as one top executive told me, "And then, magic happens."

But there tends to be a gulf between the creation of plans and the execution of plans. We assume somehow that magic will transport us across this gulf. The fact is that hard work is the only viable means of successfully linking plans to execution. This may seem elementary; it is, in fact, basic.

Maintaining Commitment and Action

This section illustrates the delusion of just having to execute in the context of three examples. The first focuses on organizations where maintaining commitment and action are particularly difficult. The second deals with organizations where planning without execution is prevalent. Finally, we consider how this delusion affects companies where long-term plans are central to their futures.

Dealing with Details

I have taken my turn as the leader of several volunteer organizations and have served as a consultant to many others. Planning sessions in such organizations are often idiosyncratic. Typically, planning groups struggle to make sure that everyone's personal agenda is represented in the plan. The result is usually a plan that is far too ambitious for the resources available.

This problem is seldom evident at the time because the planning team typically includes fifteen to twenty-five talented and creative people who are full of ideas. However, only one or two of these people are paid staff, and the rest have other things to do, such as earn a living. Thus, most of the talent and creativity in the room is unavailable most of the time.

Nevertheless, great concepts and plans usually emerge. Next comes execution. The one or two staff members can, at most, coordinate efforts and provide expertise as problems occur. The volunteers who came up with many of the ideas cannot devote enough time to implementing them.

This situation reminds me of a comment reputedly made by Will Rogers when he was asked how the Allies should deal with the German U-boat threat during World War I. He suggested that the solution was simple. You just boil the oceans. The U-boats will turn pink and pop to the top of the water. Then, you just pick them off. When asked how he would boil the oceans, he responded, "I never worry about details."

The problem is that execution *is* details. Dealing with details requires resources that volunteer organizations may not have. Thus, plans do not get executed, or their execution is so poor that expectations are far from being met. Repeated disappointments often lead volunteers to shift their commitments to other activities and other organizations.

The obvious solution to this problem is to address the five questions posed earlier. The result will be that the organization will have fewer goals and plans but will have the resources to execute. This seems straightforward—and it is—but there may be a price to pay. People usually join a volunteer organization because of a personal agenda rather than a general commitment. If the organization they join does not continue to pursue any of the items on their personal agendas, people tend to leave. Consequently, volunteer organizations that focus in order to execute will usually lose some of those members whose agenda items are outside the narrowed focus.

However, focused execution will eventually attract new members if the focus that is chosen is appealing. This choice, therefore, should be made carefully. You should take pains to balance the sure loss of a portion of your constituency against a possible gain of members due to the better execution of more focused plans. Put simply, this decision should be approached with careful strategic thinking.

Planning Without Execution

I have served on numerous government advisory committees and worked with several agencies. Many of these efforts were focused on planning or on assessing plans. The government does a substantial amount of planning.

Execution, however, is another thing. Many plans are never implemented. Many are preempted as they are being implemented. A major source of these execution problems is the frequent change of leadership that results from both our political process and, within the Department of Defense, the practice of rotating military leaders every three years or so.

I recall a planning workshop that I conducted with one agency a few years ago. During the last day of the workshop, we focused on defining measures that could be monitored to ensure that a plan was being implemented successfully. I asked those present what they currently measured for their existing plans. The participants looked at each other, not knowing what to say.

I restated my question. "Once you complete your plans and are in the implementation phase, what do you measure to assure that implementation is proceeding satisfactorily?" Still no responses. Finally, I asked, "What do you do once you have completed your plans?"

The simple answer was, "We start the next set of plans!" People went on to explain that there was no implementation phase in the way I was discussing it. The activities pursued after the planning were pretty much the same as those pursued before the planning.

One of my colleagues was the number-two executive at another government agency for two years. During one of my trips to Washington, I stopped by to say hello. I was interested in finding out what it was like to hold such a position. He told me that, at the request of the president, he had just completed a plan to substantially increase the agency's budget. That sounded exciting to me. He then said, "Unfortunately, OMB (Office of Management and Budget) zeroed out the whole increase." I asked him what his next step was. He replied that he would repeat the whole planning exercise for the following year.

Elaborate plans that are never implemented are common for government agencies. Even though some plans do lead to important changes, most planning does not result in change at all. Most plans are, in fact, just very time-consuming proposals. Only a small number of proposals make it through the political gauntlet that precedes approval and, subsequently, funding for implementation.

This process exacts a high price from people working in government agencies. They are frequently asked to prepare plans for new initiatives—to enthusiastically commit their talents and energies to creating these plans, knowing that the chances of their ever being implemented are slim.

With a bit of experience, they also learn that the chances of success are unrelated to the quality of the plans. Political trade-offs and budget deals dominate decision making. Any particular individual's detailed plan usually becomes one bullet point on one of the viewgraphs in a presentation to decision makers.

This situation leads to a special case of the delusion of just having to execute. The perception is that getting a plan approved and funded is the whole game. Execution is no big deal (even though it seldom happens). The result is that garnering budgets rather than producing results dominates the activities of agency executives.

The effects of this game on lower-level managers and bench-level workers is pervasive. They often feel that their attempts to contribute to quality plans do not matter. They become accustomed to not executing. Cynicism is common. Morale obviously suffers. This is often the price an organization pays when it succumbs to the delusion of just having to execute.

Preempted Execution

Many of the companies with whom I work are technology-based in the sense that proprietary technologies, which underlie both products and processes, are key elements of their competitive positions. Consequently, they must invest in R&D efforts to extend existing technologies and create new ones. This need is both recognized and accepted throughout these companies.

However, many R&D plans encounter execution problems. These difficulties are not due to any lack of skills and abilities on the part of the people involved. Instead, the source of these problems is the number of distractions by operational issues that consume a large portion of the attention of staff members responsible for R&D.

On countless occasions, I have called customers to ask about the status of technology development plans that I had helped them create and found that little progress was being made. Typically, the key personnel were, for instance, dealing with a customer's problem in Japan or a manufacturing problem in Germany. As a result, the R&D effort was on hold.

Another common distraction involves extended efforts by R&D organizations to get close to their internal customers. This is an excellent tactic in general. However, when it results in R&D personnel getting little if any time for R&D, the tactic undermines the overall strategy. In some cases, the R&D staff members become, in effect, staff augmentation for operational units. The operational units may be happy, but the R&D function ceases.

The overall result of distractions like these is that R&D plans aren't executed. The delusion that we just have to execute takes over. The fact that they are not executing does not seem important because they feel they will get to it soon. However, months slip by and little is accomplished. The big problem, of course, is that competitors may have been executing in earnest, while their own R&D plans were on hold.

Just having to execute is usually a much bigger issue than people perceive because execution, especially of longer-term plans, is so easily preempted by near-term problems and concerns. One near-term issue follows another. Much more quickly than you might imagine, the long term is here. However, the technology that you were counting on is not ready. You suffer the consequences of succumbing to the delusion of just having to execute.

Summary

Execution problems are pervasive. Volunteer organizations tend to be over-committed and cannot execute due to a lack of resources. Lack of execution is intrinsic to much of the planning of government agencies. Businesses are often distracted by near-term issues, and longer-term plans encounter halting execution.

Rather than "just" having to execute, the fact is that execution is often a major problem. These execution problems mean that the resources invested in planning aren't good investments. Just as important, execution problems can engender heightened levels of skepticism and cynicism in organizations and undermine their commitments to planning.

Central Principles

Exhibit 11.1 lists several execution principles drawn from the discussions in this chapter. The sustained and committed execution of plans is often difficult and is a pervasive problem in many

---

Exhibit 11.1. Execution Principles.

- Sustained and committed execution of plans can be very difficult to achieve.

- A common problem is over-commitment that results in a lack of people and financial resources for execution.

- Individual and organizational priorities dominated by near-term issues often preempt execution.

- Lack of individual and organizational commitments to plans often hinders execution.

- Without a champion—someone committed to a plan's success—plans almost always wither on the vine.

- Dealing in detail with the who, how, what, when, and why questions of plan execution is the key to avoiding the delusion of "just" having to execute.

- Hard work is the only viable means of successfully linking plans to execution.

organizations. Consequently, just having to execute becomes a delusion.

Most organizations are lean, having spent the last ten years delayering, downsizing, and rightsizing. The result is often a lack of people and financial resources for executing the plans the organization has created. Resource needs should be addressed as part of planning.

Organizations' time horizons are often compressed, with near-term issues dominating priorities. This tends to lead to resources originally committed to long-term plans being preempted by today's problems and opportunities. Subsequently, long-term plans remain perpetually long term because of the lack of progress.

Plans that are good ideas in general encounter execution problems when individuals and organizations do not find them compelling in particular. Every plan needs a champion—someone totally committed to the plan's success. Without the energy and emotion provided by champions, plans tend to get preempted at the first sign of trouble.

Plan execution needs detailed attention. Specifically, the who, how, what, when, and why questions posed earlier in this chapter need to be seriously addressed. This usually requires a substantial amount of work—which is the only way to bridge the gulf between planning and execution.

Key Questions

The delusion of just having to execute results from the misconception that planning is difficult and execution is easy. However, there are many pitfalls of execution that require substantial work to avoid. Exhibit 11.2 lists several questions to help you with this work. The questions were gleaned from the principles just discussed.

The essence of the delusion discussed in this chapter is *not* concerned with the activities associated with plan execution. Instead, this delusion emerges from the idea that execution will be straightforward—you just have to do it. However, resource constraints, skewed priorities, and a variety of types of distractions lead to execution problems. Dealing with resource, priority, and distraction issues is the key to ensuring plan execution.

Exhibit 11.2. Maintaining Commitment and Action.

- How frequently does the "ball get dropped" in your organization?
- Do you have the people and financial resources to execute your plans successfully?
- Do near-term problems and opportunities frequently preempt long-term plans and undermine progress?
- Who are the champions for your organization's long-term plans, and are they focused on executing these plans?
- Have you done the hard work of answering the who, how, what, when, and why questions of plan execution?

Most organizations, especially creative ones, formulate many compelling plans that often portend substantial competitive advantages and appealing sales and profits. However, most of these plans are never executed, and their benefits are never realized. To avoid experiencing these unfortunate consequences, you must avoid the delusion of just having to execute.

Part Four

Expect the Unexpected

We Found It Was Easy
Making Sure You Don't Skip the Hard Part

Good planning involves change. Great planning can result in fundamental change. Some changes, such as new market offerings and subsequent sales and profits, are obvious and expected. Even though these expected changes may be desirable, plan implementation often leads to other types of changes that are more fundamental and longlasting. These changes are not usually expected.

This chapter and the next focus on how to expect the unexpected. In this chapter, I discuss the two types of fundamental organizational changes that frequently emerge in the course of changing market directions: (1) the need to become a different type of organization in order to accomplish your original goals and (2) the need to change to take advantage of unexpected opportunities.

The next chapter addresses the fact that plans seldom succeed as they were planned. Success often includes an element of serendipity. It is important to develop the ability to discriminate relatively infrequent serendipity from fairly frequent diversions. Strategic thinking is an important component of that ability.

I often ask executives and senior managers about their past experiences with planning in order to help them understand the full impact of plans that are successfully executed. Occasionally, people respond by noting the sales and profits achieved as a result of successfully implementing plans. More often, however, they talk about other types of changes that occurred—typically changes they did not anticipate.

In many cases, these changes involved fundamental modifications of their organizations, the need for which they did not recognize until implementation was well along. These modifications tended to involve two related types of changes: (1) internal functional changes and (2) changes to the organization's external perspective. Both required hard work—much harder work than they had anticipated.

Internal changes included such things as new approaches to marketing and sales, finance and accounting, product support, and incentives and rewards. Basically, they came to the realization that they had to redesign themselves to become the kind of organization that could achieve the market objectives they were pursuing. This required accepting the hard fact that their old organization was not a good match with their new objectives. Most organizations find it difficult to accept this conclusion.

The other type of change concerned the ways in which they viewed their markets. Most organizations have belief systems—usually tacit—about customers, service, cost, performance, technology, innovation, and so on. These belief systems are almost always retained, despite new organizational directions. Even though a company is trying to sell new products and services in new markets, it will tend to keep its old belief system. (I discuss this at length in *Catalysts for Change* [1993].)

The result tends to be that companies have erroneous but unstated assumptions about customers' needs and preferences. For example, past customers may have wanted innovation at any price and may not have required much service. New customers may be risk averse and cost sensitive and may expect much hand holding. Approaching the latter types of customers with the former set of assumptions results in frustration for everyone involved.

Expecting the unexpected means looking for two types of new insights. First, you have to expect that your current organization will not match your new objectives. You will not initially understand the nature of the mismatch, so you should zealously look for signs of ongoing activities that do not support your goals and for missing activities that are needed to achieve your goals.

Second, your initial view of your future marketplace in general and customers in particular is likely to be heavily biased by the nature of your past markets and customers. The nature of these biases and their implications cannot be fully anticipated. Therefore, you should look for signals that reflect erroneous assumptions. When you notice that customers are confused or find your proposals difficult to believe, you are seeing examples of strong signals. More subtle signals include, for instance, questions from customers that seem almost irrelevant.

Thus recognizing the unexpected requires two types of vigilance. Adapting to the unexpected requires additional skills. The organizational changes dictated by this recognition will undoubtedly be much greater than people in your organization had anticipated. If you carefully explain your insights and their implications, people may agree with you in principle. However, they may not be fully supportive.

For example, many people who vocally support the necessary changes will unknowingly thwart these changes without realizing that their behavior is inconsistent with their stated intentions. They may be driven by old mental models that need to be changed if they are to support new directions.

Organizational culture and inertia can thwart change. Many implicit values and priorities will become evident as they clash with new requirements. For example, I have repeatedly experienced situations in which technical expertise was becoming a means to improved quality and better service rather than an end in itself. Despite this stated intention, arguments for technical correctness often emerged to counter what were perceived as unreasonable customer preferences.

Dealing with the unexpected requires looking for signs and signals that indicate the need for underlying changes. As you make these changes, you must avoid slipping into old patterns of behavior. Deciding that change is needed is much easier than sustaining the new behavior that change implies. The difficulty of this task is often a central element of the unexpected.

Making Sure You Don't Skip the Hard Part

To illustrate the delusion that change is easy, my examples in this section will be of product development, where change in the marketplace is intrinsic to the activity, and of the reinvention of organizations, where the extent of necessary change is often underestimated.

Beyond Fishing Poles

For the past fifteen years, I have been involved in a wide variety of efforts to develop computer-based products to support people who perform planning and design tasks. The targeted users range from executives and managers planning new business strategies to designers of aircraft cockpits and nuclear power plant control rooms. Several of these products continue to be part of ongoing product lines. Others remain "one off" solutions to a particular customer's planning or design problem.

When my company was developing these products, our goal was to support users who were trying to formulate the structure and content of the solution to a business or technical problem. We invested considerable effort in determining the types of structures and content that best fit the planning and design tasks of interest. Once we had devised structures and content that worked—and that users found appealing—we felt that the most difficult part of product development was over.

We were wrong. What we had at that point was a technically *valid* solution to users' planning or design problems. What remained to be demonstrated was whether or not we had an *acceptable* and *viable* solution. By *acceptable,* I mean a solution that is compatible with users' work context. *Viable* refers to the benefits of a solution being sufficiently greater than its costs—monetary and otherwise—so users and their organizations are compelled to adopt it.

Put simply, we had to provide a product that solved a customer's problem in a way that fit into the customer's context for a price the customer would find manageable. This led to substantial efforts to understand the economic, organizational, and social contexts of our targeted users. We needed to understand how our tools could enhance their jobs and how they could fit into overall business processes.

We also had to understand the costs of adopting our solutions. Many customers told us that the purchase price of the tools was only a small portion of the overall price of success. This price was dominated by the costs of getting their people up the learning curve and fully competent in the use of the tools. This led us to offer training and consulting services to accelerate learning.

I detail many of the lessons we learned in this area in *Best Laid Plans* (1994). Suffice it to say here that the extent of the issues we had to address was unexpected. Determining the technical validity of the solution was not the hard part. Carefully balancing validity, acceptability, and viability was the hard part. That was key to creating products that truly solve users' planning and design problems.

This example illustrates the need to expect the unexpected in terms of an external view of market needs and preferences. The market signs and signals were very clear: we were not meeting sales goals. Our subsequent changes led to another unexpected outcome. Although we originally expected sales to be 90 percent software and 10 percent service, we found that 50 percent of each was the outcome. Beyond fishing poles, we had to provide fishing classes and fishing trips to ensure that our customers would realize the full benefits of their purchase.

Old Wine in New Bottles

The past decade of delayering, downsizing, and rightsizing has not been limited to the private sector. Government organizations have also gotten leaner. The result has been the realignment of many organizations, as well as the consolidation of others, as numerous facilities have been targeted for closure.

This process has been accelerated for military-related government organizations due to the end of the Cold War. With traditional threats substantially diminished has come a scramble for relevance, and military organizations have tried to prove their value in a variety of ways. One approach emphasizes "dual use." Specifically, technology-oriented agencies have argued that investments in their R&D organizations result in both technology for military applications and many spin-offs for commercial applications. Thus, despite the diminished military threat, investments in these agencies are, they assert, a good bet.

Another approach emphasizes the unique nature of these agencies. They claim world class status, in part because they are the only people pursuing certain types of R&D. The point is, of course, that a unique asset should be preserved because it would be difficult, or at least expensive, to re-create.

Yet another approach is to argue that an organization's value added is more valuable—and perhaps less expensive—than that of sibling organizations. Thus, if downsizing must occur, perhaps by way of outsourcing, it should not happen in that organization. The difficulty, of course, is that everyone is trying to make the same case.

These three approaches represent different ways of repackaging the same organization. The goal is to get constituents to value the same organization in new ways. The only change occurring is in the labels and the story line. If successful, everyone gets to continue doing what they have been doing.

Some approaches, in contrast, attempt to make real change. For instance, technology-oriented government organizations in both the United States and abroad have tried more proactive approaches. One U.S. example is the Cooperative Research and Development Agreement (CRDA) program, which has resulted in numerous government-industry partnerships focused on particular technology opportunities.

I have seen even more aggressive international programs to commercialize technologies developed with government investments. In some cases, such close government-industry relationships have been longstanding elements of the socioeconomic system. In others, the relationships have emerged out of the necessity of substantially decreased R&D budgets.

Proactive approaches remove barriers and in some cases provide incentives for commercial applications of typically military technologies. Thus, rather than waiting for dual use to happen on its own, these approaches attempt to expedite the process. The goal, as noted earlier, is to raise the perceived value added of these government organizations and thereby engender increased constituency support for their continued existence.

However, most of these organizations have not been expecting the unexpected. In this case, the unexpected has been the extent of the mismatch between the entrepreneurial environment typically needed for commercialization of new technologies and the government's organizational processes and culture. Put simply, dealing with the government imposes much more overhead than most commercial organizations are willing to accept. Also, the government is ill-equipped to foster serious dual use. Realizing substantial, albeit indirect, commercial returns from government investments in R&D requires that government systems be designed to achieve this goal. To the extent that such returns continue to be weakly nurtured by-products of investments made for different purposes, these returns will continue to be, at best, minimal.

The goal of reinventing government agencies may just be another way of trying to decrease the cost of government. If, however, it is truly a desire to change the role and nature of government—at least in some areas—then the organizations involved have to avoid skipping the hard part of change. They need to redesign their processes to match their new objectives.

More Change Than Expected

As government R&D organizations have scrambled for relevance, one of their primary constituents has also had to scramble. Academia, which includes universities and related academic institutions, has certainly felt the tightening of the federal R&D budget belt. The result has been the revisiting of goals, strategies, and plans.

An outgrowth of this process has been substantially increased efforts to recruit industry benefactors. For annual membership fees and sponsorship of specific projects, companies are able to collaborate with faculty and graduate students in pursuing research of mutual interest. In spite of a variety of tensions between the worldviews of academia and business, many people have muddled through these tensions and created productive relationships.

Despite this bit of progress, little real change has occurred. Strategic planning may result in new clusters of faculty and graduate students, as well as new labels for these clusters, but the overall system remains unchanged. For example, faculty have to pursue promotion and tenure based on the longstanding practice of judging people solely on the basis of their individual accomplishments.

Universities thought that selling university-industry partnerships would be the hard part of change. They did not expect that making these partnerships work is actually the hard part. Making them work requires rethinking the universities' processes ranging from finance and accounting to incentives and rewards. In other words, they did not expect to have to adapt to their new markets.

Universities are also facing challenges as they try to adapt in educational markets. The apprentice approach to graduate education is expensive and time consuming, which makes it difficult to attract people who have already tasted the benefits of professional jobs. This has led many companies to create their own university-type training.

Technology is enabling distance learning, which allows people to take courses at sites remote from the university. This raises the possibility that every physics student in the country could attend the lectures of the best physics teacher. Beyond dramatically reducing the need for physics faculty, this would substantially reduce the need for bricks and mortar, which is usually a strong suit of traditional academic institutions.

The unexpected for universities is the likely need to substantially redesign themselves. The design of the new university was recently a topic of several rounds of Internet-based discussion with several of my long-term colleagues around the country. These discussions exposed a wide variety of perspectives. At one extreme, people advocated the need to eventually adopt a complete business model in terms of markets, products, channels, technologies, and so forth. At the other extreme, people argued for returning to the nineteenth-century European model that is focused on the pure pursuit of knowledge. The strong nature of the interchanges in these discussions suggested to me that the emergence of the new university will involve many long debates.

Universities are not the only academic institutions facing the challenge to change. The National Research Council (NRC)— the operating arm of the National Academy of Sciences, National Academy of Engineering, and Institute of Medicine—is an example of an organization that operates very much like a university, at least in comparison to government or industry. The National Academy of Science was founded in 1863 by President Lincoln to provide advice to the government on scientific and technical matters.

The NRC is usually the agent of this advice. At any one time, there are typically 1,000 ongoing committees and study panels, composed of roughly 10,000 volunteers, pursuing assessments of the scientific and technical state of the art on issues ranging from nutrition to home medical devices to air traffic control systems. The product is usually a carefully worded and thoroughly reviewed report containing recommendations to the government organization that commissioned the study.

As government budgets for studies—and everything else—have tightened, the NRC has been urged to adapt to the same pressures being faced by government agencies. For example, the standing committee that I currently chair has been pressured to produce its reports and recommendations in a much more timely manner—in four to six months rather than two to three years. This is difficult to accomplish when much of the content of reports is generated by volunteer experts, and all of this content must undergo a rigorous review. Further, without these experts and this review process, the NRC's credibility might be severely compromised.

The unexpected for our committee was the simple fact that just doing the same old things a bit better would be an inadequate response to our constituency. We needed a new type of product to supplement our traditional products. The result was a workshop series targeted at agencies' key issues or emerging national issues. The proceedings of these workshops are written by a professional editor based on transcripts recorded during the workshops. No "official" recommendations are made, hence the review process is much quicker. The result is a slim, well-written product that appears in a matter of months.

I expect that more unexpected challenges are waiting in the wings. For instance, traditions that the NRC has nurtured for more than 130 years may have to change substantially if the organization is to fully respond to the challenges faced by its government sponsors. For example, slowly emerging recommendations by august groups may have to be replaced by much more modest but relatively quick observations in rapidly moving areas such as the Internet. Otherwise, the NRC could become a nonplayer in such hot areas.

However, long-held beliefs and traditions are very difficult to change. The NRC and many universities have, to varying extents, succumbed to the delusion that adapting their products to the marketplace is the hard part. However, adapting their processes so they can truly excel with these new products is actually the hard part. They should not skip it.

Summary

The vignettes in this section have illustrated the delusion of thinking the hard part is over—that the rest is easy—when in fact it has just begun. The hard part of developing new products in not just creating a technically valid solution to customers' needs. Ensuring that the solution is acceptable and viable within the context of customers' environments is the most difficult factor in gaining market success.

Beyond adapting solutions to fully meet customers' needs, you have to adapt your organization to achieve high levels of effectiveness in providing these new solutions. Organizations seldom expect that they will have to redesign *themselves,* rather than solely their products and services. Consequently, when this need eventually emerges, it can be very difficult to make the necessary changes.

Central Principles

Exhibit 12.1 lists several expectation principles drawn from the discussions in this chapter. Good planning involves change, and the hard part is actually making the changes rather than just planning the changes. Great plans tend to involve fundamental changes in your organization to solve a problem or take advantage of an opportunity in your marketplace.

The delusion of having already accomplished the hard part stems from the failure to recognize the nature of the fundamental changes required for success. This, in turn, is often due to the difficulty of recognizing these needs prior to implementation. As a consequence, you have to be vigilant to spot these needs as implementation proceeds.

Once you reach this recognition, you are likely to face the difficulty of having to accept the fact that your old organization is not a good match with your new objectives. Then you will have to deal with the natural tendency of organizations to maintain old belief systems despite intentions to sell new products and services in new markets. Changing belief systems involves first making them explicit and then constructively articulating and reinforcing the new belief system.

The unexpected often includes the market's less-than-enthusiastic reactions to products and services that are technically valid but not matched to the context of use and do not provide benefits that exceed the cost of purchase and use. Failures of technically valid

---

Exhibit 12.1. Execution Principles.

- Good planning involves change. Great planning can result in fundamental change.

- Fundamental changes in your environment require fundamental changes in your organization.

- You may not recognize the need for fundamental changes of your organization until implementation is well along.

- You may have to accept the hard fact that your old organization is not a good match with your new objectives.

- Even though a company is trying to sell new products and services in new markets, it will tend to keep its old belief system. This tends to result in frustration for everyone involved.

- You have to provide products and services that solve customers' problems in ways that fit into customers' context and for prices customers find manageable.

- The technical validity of solutions is not the hard part. Instead, the careful balancing of validity, acceptability, and viability issues is the key to creating products that truly solve users' problems.

- Deciding which changes are needed is much easier than sustaining the new behavior that the changes require.

---

products due to acceptability and viability problems are common. Avoiding such consequences involves planning for acceptability and viability while instituting mechanisms for detecting such problems when they inevitably emerge as customers use the product.

The delusion that change is easy is due to the simple fact that planning change is so much easier than implementing it. Implementation is very difficult and fraught with pitfalls. The biggest pitfall is not being able to deal with the unexpected. However, once you accept the fact that the unexpected will happen—and develop mechanisms for recognizing it when it does happen—you are much less likely to succumb to the delusion that change is easy.

Key Questions

The delusion that change is easy stems from not anticipating the true difficulties of implementation. Often there is such relief that plans are finally finished that people assume implementation will be straightforward. The questions in Exhibit 12.2 will help you avoid this assumption. The questions are based on the expectation principles just discussed.

The essence of the delusion discussed in this chapter is *not* concerned with the need to be clairvoyant so that nothing unexpected will happen. The delusion is that there will be no surprises. However, surprise is intrinsic to fundamental change. The more you ignore this possibility, the more you will be surprised.

The key is to create the mind-set and the mechanisms for recognizing and responding to the unexpected. Although you may not know what to expect, you certainly can expect to encounter problems and opportunities that you had not anticipated. With the right mind-set and mechanisms, you will have more opportunities than problems.

Exhibit 12.2. Making Sure You Don't Skip the Hard Part.

- Does it seem like the rest will be easy once you have finished your plans for your organization's new directions?

- Are you prepared to deal with the fundamental organizational changes that may become necessary as you execute these plans?

- Are you prepared to deal with validity, acceptability, or viability problems that are likely to emerge as customers react to your new products and services?

- Have you created mechanisms for detecting and recognizing needs for the types of changes likely to appear unexpectedly?

- As the change process evolves, is your organization likely to need tuning, repair, or wholesale change?

We Succeeded as We Planned
Placing Yourself in the Path of Serendipity

A couple of years ago, I was near the end of a planning session with a mid-sized telecommunications company. We had sketched out several very ambitious plans. I turned to the CEO and asked, "Do you expect all these plans to succeed?" The whole top management team looked at him, waiting to see what he would say. He responded, "I hope not. If all our plans succeed, we aren't being aggressive enough."

You should expect many of your plans to fail in the sense that they do not lead to the consequences you anticipated when you created them. More important, you should expect that your *successful* plans usually will not succeed in the ways you anticipated. Expecting the unexpected involves embracing the reality that plans—especially successful plans—seldom work out in the ways you expect.

What then is the purpose of the plans? As I discuss in great detail in *Best Laid Plans* (1994), the purpose of planning—and of plans—is to place you in the path of serendipity. Planning helps you clarify your goals and alternative strategies for achieving these goals. Planning should sensitize you and everyone else involved to the factors most likely to influence success.

Consider your greatest past successes. Why did they happen? What were the success factors? If your answer is that successes were mostly due to great plans flawlessly executed, your experiences are unusual. Most other people of whom I have asked this question responded with stories of success factors emerging in unlikely ways and in unanticipated places.

Once you accept the probability that success often involves an important element of serendipity, you can prepare for this possibility. For example, in your planning you can entertain scenarios that seem highly improbable but portray factors that would be highly desirable if they were to emerge. This will prime you to recognize these factors when and if they do emerge in unanticipated ways.

The potential role of serendipity also affects the ways you execute plans. If you expect that your plans will ultimately be executed in unexpected ways, you will be open to serendipity. You will know the success factors for which you are looking and be open to seeing them when they arise. In contrast, people suffering from the delusion that success will occur exactly as planned tend not to see success factors unless they arrive in patterns that match their plans.

An important principle is that good planning enables you to succeed in ways other than the way you planned. Good planning fosters sensitivity to the true conditions for success. It also helps you understand the wealth of ways in which these conditions can emerge. Good plans, therefore, enable you to execute while also being flexible and open to adapting plans to new situations.

Good plans play a critical role in this flexibility. Without good plans, every phone call and customer contact will seem to be a potential opportunity. In fact, the vast majority—99 percent or more—of these events are just diversions. Occasionally, an event represents a true opportunity—an instance of serendipity. Good plans let you say no to the countless diversions that beg for attention each day and yes when opportunity is really at the door.

Placing Yourself in the Path of Serendipity

Three vignettes in this section illustrate the role of serendipity in success and show how you can place yourself in its path. The first example focuses on research and development (R&D) where serendipitous payoffs rather than intended returns are quite common. The other examples show how serendipity can affect both the nature of your products and the markets you pursue.

Investing in the Unknown

Strategic thinking about R&D presents a dilemma. Choices among R&D investments are usually driven by long-term intentions regarding products and services, including competitive advantages important to succeeding with these market offerings. However, experienced—and realistic—R&D managers and investors know that many investments do not produce the desired advantages. Further, the advantages that are created are often unexpected.

My company recently completed a study for a government agency of a long-term R&D program. This program, now in its twentieth year, was established with a goal of improving the design of aircraft cockpits. Participants in this program included most U.S. military aircraft manufacturers and several smaller leading-edge, high-tech companies.

We interviewed a wide variety of people involved in the program, asking them about what was produced and what happened to these products. Government interviewees told us about the official "deliverables." These products, in our assessment, fell a bit short of original expectations for the program. Further, adoption for use in cockpit design has been minimal to date.

Interviews with the companies involved in the program revealed a whole different side of the story. Most of the smaller high-tech firms involved in the program had leveraged the knowledge and skills gained in this effort to create new software products for other government customers, as well as commercial markets. Thus, there were many valuable by-products of this R&D investment.

From some perspectives, the overall value of the by-products of this R&D program exceeded the value of the intended products. According to R&D executives and senior managers in numerous industries, this is not uncommon. The surprises—the serendipitous implications of results—often seem to provide the biggest payoff.

In another study, we interviewed senior R&D executives, asking them to identify a success story and a failure story. We used a structured interview format to assess the underlying factors that differentiate success from failure. Of particular relevance to our discussion here—and a serendipitous finding for us—was a story that was a success story for an executive in one agency and a failure story for another executive in a different agency. In other words, the same story was about both success and failure.

How is this possible? The failure occurred when the intended results of the R&D investment did not materialize for the agency making the original investment. The success followed when another agency, seeing technology that was now available, applied it in a completely different domain with impressive results. One organization's trash became another's treasure.

When a government agency is involved, this result can be reasonable. The return on investment discussed earlier did not happen as it was intended. Nevertheless, it did happen. The bottom line on the government's investment income statement looks fine. Of course, if the organizations involved had been two different businesses, this transfer of returns would be far from palatable.

Why invest in an effort that pays off for somebody else? Stated differently, how can you ensure that more of the serendipitous payoffs are yours rather than those of your competitors? The answer is to avoid the delusion that you will succeed as planned. As you execute your plan, you must remain sensitive to succeeding in ways other than those you expect.

You must vigorously execute your plans while remaining vigilant for cues that other paths might provide higher payoffs. This is difficult to do well, especially for one person to do well. How can you keep your nose to the grindstone and still watch for serendipity? Isn't this a prescription for getting a bruised nose?

One way to deal with this dilemma is to have some people grinding and others watching the horizon. Another approach is to have regular "assumption bashing" meetings where your many assumptions are identified and challenged. The key is to find a mechanism that combines day-to-day vigorous execution of plans with regular reality checks to avoid the delusion that you will succeed just as you planned.

Making a Few Very Strong Connections

For thirty years, I have been intrigued with the possibility of embodying engineering methods in computer-based tools. My earliest effort involved computerizing reliability and maintainability methods. In this case, the tool was a deck of punched cards, with data cards for each analysis appended to the back of the deck. My next effort focused on computerizing network flow analysis methods for use on a time-shared computer, fortunately minus the deck of cards.

In the last ten years, more and more applications have come into use for engineering work stations and microcomputers. These typically have Microsoft Windows running on desktop computers; occasionally, but less and less, Macintosh applications are used. The quest is still development of computer-based methods for analysis, modeling, planning, and design. Whatever the platform, my company's approach to conceptualizing and developing our tools is very much market-driven. We first identify people's planning and design needs in a particular domain (for example, automobile design) and then determine the methods and technologies that can best meet these needs. This process usually leads to a long wish list of desired functions and capabilities for the new tool.

For one of our tools, we decided to provide everything on the wish list; we included everything that anybody had requested. This tool was overwhelming. People had great difficulty navigating among all the options and features. The tool was a failure.

We quickly went back to the drawing board. We slimmed down the tool so that it only included the basic set of functions that everybody said they wanted. This shift from doing everything that anybody wanted to doing only the basic things that everybody wanted resulted in a successful tool. It is now in use at many companies and in other types of enterprises.

When we pursue a tool development effort, we usually have a sense of what is needed. We create what is termed a *look and feel prototype,* which serves as a vehicle to prompt comments and suggestions from potential users. Typically, we are inundated with ideas.

Serendipity often emerges at this point. Among the wealth of comments and suggestions are usually a few nuggets—wonderful ideas that will provide great benefits to users. Most of the suggestions, however, are just reasonable ideas that would be diversions from our goals of delighting users with the new tool.

The key to placing yourself in the path of serendipity is the ability to recognize it when it happens. You need to be able to let the world of ideas and potential opportunities wash over you and spot the one or two things that will really make a difference. This requires that you have a well-tuned filter based on a clear set of goals and plans.

You should not try to respond to every idea and potential opportunity that the world offers. If you do, you are likely to experience the same failure we experienced when we tried to do everything that anybody wanted. You are looking for a few very strong connections between your original intentions and new ways of achieving these goals. That's serendipity.

Doing What You Really Should

For many years, our planning and design tools were targeted at technically oriented users, typically, engineers working with people from marketing and finance to plan new market offerings. New product planning predominated the projects we undertook.

In the late 1980s, customers started asking us how our methods and tools might be applied to overall business planning, including analyzing market opportunities, identifying and developing channels, and competitive benchmarking. These inquiries led to new tools and systems that became the mainstay of our business.

Our first software tool of this type focused on strategic planning in the sense of creating an integrated plan for how markets, products, and technologies fit together across markets and channels. This tool also enabled integration of subordinate plans for manufacturing, service, and R&D. In addition, the outputs of our product planning tool could serve as key inputs to the strategic planning tool.

This first step in the direction of business systems was well received by our customers. However, by listening carefully, we identified several shortfalls. We needed to be able to support strategic thinking for those elements of corporate strategy that go beyond products and services. For example, people wanted to be supported in thinking about the overall relationship of their company to its markets—both current and emerging relationships. This led to a new software tool focused on situation assessment using case studies and a knowledge base gleaned from the experiences of nearly two hundred companies in the transportation, computer, and defense industries.

Another shortfall concerned people's abilities to access data about markets, competitors, products, and technologies. It is impossible to create an off-the-shelf software tool that provides immediate access to a variety of proprietary corporate databases. There has to be some tailoring to integrate data sources and provide appropriate methods of manipulating and presenting information. To meet this need, therefore, we had to expand our offerings to include custom software services.

A third critical shortfall involved the difficulties of implementing plans. Despite the potential for creating first-rate plans with our various software tools, if these plans are not successfully implemented, we have not met the customers' needs. This recognition—prompted by many comments and suggestions by customers—led to the development of new methods and tools for diagnosing companies' abilities to implement plans, as well as underlying barriers to implementation. The result was one new product and several new services.

Thus, we identified three shortcomings of our offerings and created new products and services to meet these additional needs. While this may sound straightforward, it was not. Our customers and colleagues offered countless suggestions, many of which started with, "You know what you really should be doing?" There was no lack of possibilities.

This is usually the case when you place yourself in the path of serendipity. Traffic is usually heavy on such paths. In our case, we had to watch for possibilities to support key elements of strategic thinking. We also had to consider how our competencies in methods and tools, as well as new competencies we could imagine gaining, could provide such support. These two considerations substantially winnowed down the plethora of alternatives.

The earlier discussion of planning and design tools illustrated serendipity in identifying new ways of realizing your goals. This business systems example illustrates serendipity in the sense of identifying new goals that can be achieved using existing competencies. Both of these types of serendipity can provide tremendous opportunities.

How about both types of serendipity at the same time? In other words, does it make sense to consider new ways of achieving new goals? The answer can be yes, but it is usually very risky to do that. Developing brand new competencies to operate in brand new markets is extremely difficult. In *Start Where You Are* (Rouse, 1996), I discuss many examples of how companies have tried such changes. The success rate is very low.

Summary

The three examples in this section have illustrated three different ways in which plans may not succeed as expected. R&D investments frequently lead to unexpected payoffs—so much so that the unexpected can be expected. The discussion of software tools for planning and design showed how serendipity can affect the nature of products. The discussion of business systems, in contrast, illustrated the effects of serendipity on identifying customers and their problems.

All three examples share a very important attribute, namely, the great likelihood that plans will not succeed as intended. If you suffer from the delusion that success usually arrives as planned, you are very likely to miss opportunities for substantial success. Good plans are essential to execution, and execution is essential. As you execute, however, use the goals and strategies that underlie your plans as filters through which to view the traffic on the path of serendipity. Vigilant and intelligent monitoring of this traffic is likely to lead to new ways to succeed.

Central Principles

Exhibit 13.1 lists several serendipity principles gleaned from the earlier discussions in this chapter. Expecting the unexpected involves recognizing the likelihood that success will emerge in ways other than those you anticipate. Just as important is the recognition that this will happen only if you are open to such possibilities.

Gaining this recognition requires that you view planning in a much broader way than it is often viewed. Planning serves to clarify and articulate goals and strategies, as well as define sequences of actions that embody these goals and strategies. Beyond these basics, planning should delineate success factors and key indicators of the emergence of these factors. This will sensitize you and all involved to indicators that may presage new paths to success.

Thus, good plans support execution in pursuit of goals and strategies, while ensuring that you are open to adapting goals, strategies, and plans to evolving and new situations. Good plans also provide the basis for saying no to the many potential diversions that present themselves but yes to infrequent, but very real, opportu-

---

Exhibit 13.1. Serendipity Principles.

- Expecting the unexpected involves embracing the reality that plans—especially successful plans—seldom work out in the ways you anticipated.

- Planning helps you clarify your goals and alternative strategies for achieving these goals, while sensitizing you and everyone else involved to the factors most likely to influence success.

- Good plans enable you to execute while being flexible and open to adapting plans to new situations.

- Good plans enable saying no to the countless diversions that beg for attention each day and yes when opportunity is really at the door.

- You need to be able to let the world of ideas and potential opportunities wash over you and spot the one or two things that will really make a difference.

- You should look for a few strong connections between your original intentions and new ways of achieving these goals.

- To avoid the delusion that you will succeed just as you planned, create mechanisms that combine day-to-day vigorous execution of plans with regular reality checks.

---

nities. This is made possible by the clarity of intentions captured in good plans.

The delusion that you will succeed in the ways you plan can lead you to ignore the trends and events going on around you. This kind of concentration can be a great operational strength. It also can be a great strategic weakness. You need to pay attention to the plethora of signs and signals emanating from the marketplace. The goal, however, is not to act on all this information but to make sense of the information so you can identify and recognize the one or two things that will really make a difference.

The identification and recognition process involves being alert to a few strong connections to your original goals and strategies. Those connections relate to new ways of achieving your goals and embodying your strategies. You are not looking for opportunities in general. You are looking for possible modifications or extensions of your specific intentions.

It is easy to succumb to the delusion of success coming in the ways anticipated. To avoid this natural tendency, you need to create mechanisms that both support day-to-day execution and provide opportunities for regular reality checks. This involves checking that assumed realities still hold, as well as checking for new realities that can transform your path to success.

Key Questions

The delusion that plans will succeed—or perhaps did succeed—as expected is a natural tendency. Overcoming this delusion is necessary to ensure that you really understand the basis of your company's success. It is also necessary if you are to take advantage of the substantial opportunities of which you are, as yet, unaware. Exhibit 13.2 lists several questions to help you do this. The questions are based on the serendipity principles just discussed.

Exhibit 13.2. Placing Yourself in the Path of Serendipity.

- How often have your plans worked out exactly as intended? How often have your successes happened exactly as planned?

- Are your current plans premised on success emerging exactly as you anticipate? What if this does not happen?

- Are you monitoring signs and signals from the marketplace that can both support your expectations, if appropriate, and provide strong evidence when new paths are desirable or necessary?

- Are your plans formulated so they will support adapting to evolving or new market opportunities, including unexpected opportunities?

- What mechanisms have you created for making regular reality checks? How well have they worked in the past?

The essence of the delusion of succeeding as planned is *not* about this conclusion being wrong but about its being much too narrow. If you do not understand the real basis of past successes, you are unlikely to repeat them. Similarly, if you do not appreciate the range of ways you are likely to succeed in the future, you are unlikely to achieve the greatest success possible.

The key is to formulate clear intentions and develop an in-depth understanding of how these intentions might be realized. This understanding should sensitize you to central success factors. This understanding should also enable you to create mechanisms for monitoring the path of serendipity and spotting those infrequent, but extremely valuable, opportunities that will lead to new levels of success.

Conclusions:
Beyond Delusions

When I talk with groups of executives and senior managers about the thirteen delusions, I always get knowing looks of recognition, as well as frequent side comments and one-line jokes about their own organizations. Once the initial sense of déjà vu passes, however, people say that articulating these organizational tendencies is not enough. They want to know how to move beyond the delusions—how to unburden their strategic thinking.

I offer a three-part reply. First, the Central Principles and Key Questions at the end of each chapter provide a rich source of guidance on when and how to raise issues and how to address them. Asking the right questions at the right time can be invaluable for changing the mind-set of executives and managers.

The second part of my reply concerns who the agent of change will be. In some cases, it is the leader of the organization; in others, the leader cannot serve in this role. A facilitator is needed—either an internal or external person whose assigned task is to dispel delusions.

Third, I suggest methods and tools for improving strategic thinking. The choices of methods and tools depend on the task at hand, whether it is planning new products (Rouse, 1991, 1994), formulating business strategy (Rouse, 1992, 1994), planning organizational change (Rouse, 1993), or conducting a market assessment (Rouse, 1996). As I noted in the Preface, the value of any method or tool depends on your ability to move beyond delusions.

In this concluding section, I will discuss the role of the seventy Key Questions posed at the end of the earlier chapters; then I will consider the roles of leaders and facilitators. Finally, I reflect on the fundamental nature of the thirteen delusions and why you have to continually work to overcome your natural tendencies.

Seventy Key Questions

A list of the Key Questions posed at the end of the discussion of each delusion is shown in the Appendix. Consider these thirteen sets of questions—seventy in all—to be your emergency checklists for use when steering your organization through turbulent stretches of strategic thinking. In particular, use them when you are least able to sit back and determine for yourself which questions you should be asking.

Why do I offer questions instead of answers? Most executives and managers want answers, and they want them quickly. My philosophy is that, in almost all cases, people already have answers. They can't make good use of what they know, however, because they don't know how to ask the right questions.

Further, questions are safe. For example, I often ask questions such as, "I don't know that much about your business, but it seems to me that strategies X and Y are incompatible. I am probably just naive, but can you explain to me how these things fit together?" This always results in helpful explanations. It also frequently leads people to realize that they had not seen the underlying incompatibilities, often for reasons that I had not imagined.

It is important that your questions not be manipulative. Questions should not be seen as exams to be passed. To avoid this perception, you have to accept and reveal your own lack of knowledge. If you are the leader from within the organization, you cannot possibly know your manager's job as well as he or she does. If you are a consultant from outside the organization, you cannot know your client's business as well as your client does.

Thus, you should look for holes in your own knowledge, share them with the group, and use this sharing as a basis for asking key questions. The goal is to foster a mutual search for insights. Having mastered the material in this book, you know the Key Questions and the general nature of the answers. However, you do not know which of the delusions are most central. Of particular importance, you do not know the context-specific nature of their manifestations.

Leading Strategic Thinking

Most readers of this book are likely to be responsible for strategic planning in their organization. If you have this responsibility, you are the leader of the strategic thinking process. This section shows you how to use the book as a basis for moving beyond delusions.

As the leader, and hence a member of the planning team, you cannot deal with your group at arm's length. Any questions you raise, you have to help answer. Further, many people will expect that you, as the leader, should know the answers to many of the questions. I suggest that you work through this book before immersing yourself in planning. Review each delusion with your group. Ask yourselves the questions at the end of each chapter. Try to reach some level of agreement on the delusions most hindering your organization's progress and on how you intend to move beyond them. This should take no more than one day, especially if everyone has read the book before you start.

As you move on to the work of planning, use the compilation in the Appendix as your emergency checklists. You as the leader can be the primary monitor of the checklists, although this can be difficult if you are also leading the planning discussions. You might choose to designate one or more team members to be responsible for the checklists. A good approach is to have the whole planning team monitor them, although I often find that responsibilities given to everybody tend to be ignored.

Another alternative is to use a facilitator. This person can be from elsewhere in your organization or can be an external consultant who is assigned the duty of facilitating the planning process and monitoring the checklists. Experienced facilitators should be skilled at working with teams at both levels in this way. People without those skills will find this difficult.

Facilitating Strategic Thinking

The second largest group of readers of this book will probably be consultants who facilitate strategic planning processes for their clients. As a facilitator, your job is to help your clients think strategically and, in the process, bring together their knowledge of markets, competitors, technologies, their own organization, and so forth. Your job is also to help clients avoid the delusions discussed in this book.

I have facilitated hundreds of planning sessions with several thousand executives and senior managers. I usually know something about the organizations I work with. For example, I might know the basics of their underlying technologies. However, I am always far from being an expert. Expertise with a particular organization is not why I am hired. Clients retain me because of my broad experiences across many types of organizations and my ability to facilitate sessions that include very senior people.

Clients have often told me that good facilitation involves two levels of skill. At a basic level, a facilitator should ensure that the group follows the agreed-upon discussion and decision-making processes, which includes making sure that everyone has an opportunity to participate. It also involves ensuring that conflicts and disagreements are constructively addressed.

A higher level of facilitation involves asking questions of the group that are based on your perception of the coherence—or incoherence—of the group's progress. The earlier example of my question about the compatibility of two strategies illustrates the type of questions needed. Keep in mind the importance of asking questions without implying that you already know the answers.

Occasionally, questions have to be more aggressive. A few years ago, I was working with a poorly performing subsidiary of a major steel company. My goal was to help them design a planning process to support the creation of plans that would reinvigorate the company. After extensive interviews with each member of the top management team, I met with the whole team and suggested alternative ways to proceed.

Every alternative encountered apathy. Each idea would fail, they claimed, because of difficult market conditions, government constraints, or insensitive corporate parents. Finally, after a couple of hours of this, I stood up and said to the seated group, "What are you going to do then? Sit here and wait to be fired?" This wake-up call got people's attention, and we were able to make substantial progress.

Another time, I was working with a company that was planning a new microprocessor. We started by focusing on the nature of the market and the key trade-offs associated with different market segments. The lack of discussion of technology frustrated one senior engineer, who finally blurted out, "I just want to design this thing, not get bogged down in marketing and sales issues."

I could see that his comment hit a responsive cord with many people in the room. I said, "You're right. Let's just quit right now. You can start on your design this afternoon." The tide shifted immediately, with people saying, "We can't do that. We have to understand the market." We progressed smoothly from that point on.

Thus, your use of the questions in the Appendix needs to be tailored to the current context. In some cases, the questions can be almost rhetorical. You do not really expect the group to stop and discuss them. In other situations, you have to be much more forceful and occasionally confrontational. The former is appropriate when the group needs a reminder of its assumptions. The latter is needed when the group is seriously misleading itself.

A word of caution. My experience is that you can productively use only one or two confrontation bullets in your facilitation gun. The first bullet, if used wisely, can have a tremendous effect. The second bullet, if very carefully aimed, may also have a positive impact. However, once you get beyond two confrontations in a single planning session, you will be perceived as a confrontational person, which will undermine your value as a facilitator.

Beyond Delusions

With good leadership or facilitation—and your emergency checklists—you should be able to move beyond the thirteen delusions. You will know how to

- Challenge commonly held assumptions
- Establish goals that make a difference
- Make sure that plans lead to actions
- Expect the unexpected

In these ways, you can avoid undermining your strategic thinking.

You can do all this, but you cannot do it once and for all. It's not possible to diet, get to your desired weight, and then eat whatever you want from then on. It's not possible to exercise, achieve a desired level of fitness, and then never exercise again. Similarly, you can develop the skills to recognize and avoid delusions, but you cannot eliminate their reappearance.

The reason for this is straightforward. Jumping to solutions is a totally natural act, both psychologically and socially. In most cases, this tendency is a great strength. It means there's no need to make new plans for familiar and frequent tasks. In this way, it substantially and importantly simplifies problem solving and decision making.

However, jumping to solutions, especially after having succumbed to one or more delusions, presents major problems when you want and need to think strategically. These delusions can undermine strategic thinking to the point that results are useless at best and, at worst, dangerous to the health of your organization. Thus, the knowledge and skills for moving beyond delusions are essential to your future.

Appendix:
Seventy Key Questions

Comparing Visions and Realities

1. In what specific ways do your vision and reality differ?
2. How does the expected pace of realizing your vision compare to the actual pace?
3. Does your plan need to be modified to reflect more realistic expectations?
4. In light of current realities, what new visions are possible and likely?
5. What elements of these new visions can be incorporated into your vision?
6. Is your vision, perhaps as modified for current realities, still compelling?

Letting Go of the World Class Myth

7. Is the general feeling that all functional areas of your organization, as well as your organization as a whole, are outstanding or at least above average? Is this feeling justified?
8. Does your organization do the work necessary for achieving and maintaining preeminent capabilities in areas that provide competitive advantage?
9. From where do the important ideas in your organization come? What proportions of innovations are coming from customers, competitors, and other industries?
10. What processes do you have for identifying weaknesses in your organization, and how well do these processes work?
11. What processes do you have for remediating the deficiencies that you identify, and how well do these processes work?

Assessing Relationships with Markets

12. What signals are key to assessing your relationships with your markets?
13. What measurements do you regularly make to assess your relationships?
14. What were the real reasons for your past successes and failures?
15. What old paradigms are you in the process of abandoning, and what new paradigms are you adopting?
16. How are you balancing this parallel abandonment and adoption of paradigms?
17. What existing market relationships are key to learning how to develop the new relationships you seek?

Moving Beyond the Status Quo

18. Are you and your organization committed to goals that will really make a difference?
19. What proportion of your organization's resources is focused on maintaining and enhancing the status quo?
20. How much time do you spend leading and nurturing new directions?
21. What new efforts have you started in the past year? What efforts have you stopped?
22. Are your incentive and reward systems aligned with the changes that you seek?
23. Does your future totally depend on irrational commitments made by people willing to operate outside your organizational systems?
24. How do you support champions to work within your systems and succeed?

Overcoming Obsessions with Technical Correctness

25. Does your organization tend to focus on finding the right way, or are multiple points of view encouraged?
26. What disciplinary lenses most affect your organization's decision making?
27. What functional silos are scattered across your organizational landscape?

28. Do you convene and empower cross-functional teams to tackle important problems?
29. How do expertise and accomplishments affect earning respect in your organization?

Avoiding Chasing Purple Rhinos

30. How often have you found your organization depending on a purple rhino to solve all its problems?
31. How often have purple rhinos solved any of your fundamental problems, as opposed to simply masking them for a while longer?
32. How many of your current business opportunities can be characterized as endangered species—unlikely to contribute to repeatable, sustainable revenue?
33. How diverse is your portfolio of business relationships and opportunities? Are there numerous ways to succeed?
34. How careful and patient are you in developing and sustaining business relationships via clear and frequent value added?

Managing Conflicts of Values and Priorities

35. Have you ever thought there was a consensus only to later discover there were actually strong disagreements?
36. Can your organization agree to take action despite unresolved disagreements about elements of the action plans?
37. How often have disagreements in your organization had sources much deeper than the surface features of the disagreements?
38. What are the needs and beliefs that underlie any recent or ongoing conflicts in your organization?
39. Can you negotiate win-win solutions by scoping the set of issues to ensure that at least some needs are met for all stakeholders?

Balancing Short Term and Long Term

40. Have your short-term focus and your lack of long-term goals resulted in your being trapped in the present with little if any view of the future?
41. What recent instances are indicative of your organization's abilities to sacrifice short-term returns for potential long-term gains?

42. What investments are you making whose primary returns will be in the long term?

43. What knowledge and skills are you gaining that will provide competencies for dealing with the long term?

44. Is your long-term thinking focused on the few critical things that matter? Are you vigilantly avoiding the many possible diversions?

Navigating the Tangled Webs of Relationships

45. Who are the stakeholders that influence the success or failure of your products and services?

46. What roles do these stakeholders play, and what is the nature of their stakes?

47. Which stakeholders are primary, and which are secondary?

48. What benefits of your offerings most delight your primary stakeholders?

49. What aspects of your offerings are crucial to gaining the support of secondary stakeholders?

Avoiding Institutionalized Conflicts

50. Are your organizational processes aligned with your goals, strategies, and plans—or are they in the way?

51. Do your incentive and reward systems support execution of your strategy?

52. Do the structural relationships among organizational components support your strategy?

53. How much of your most recent reorganization was simply the changing of labels?

54. How much organizational baggage was eliminated in your most recent reorganization?

55. Do you have a transition plan for transforming your old organization and processes into the new?

Maintaining Commitment and Action

56. How frequently does the "ball get dropped" in your organization?

57. Do you have the people and financial resources to execute your plans successfully?

58. Do near-term problems and opportunities frequently preempt long-term plans and undermine progress?
59. Who are the champions for your organization's long-term plans, and are they focused on executing these plans?
60. Have you done the hard work of answering the who, how, what, when, and why questions of plan execution?

Making Sure You Don't Skip the Hard Part

61. Does it seem like the rest will be easy once you have finished your plans for your organization's new directions?
62. Are you prepared to deal with the fundamental organizational changes that may become necessary as you execute these plans?
63. Are you prepared to deal with validity, acceptability, or viability problems that are likely to emerge as customers react to your new products and services?
64. Have you created mechanisms for detecting and recognizing needs for the types of changes likely to appear unexpectedly?
65. As the change process evolves, is your organization likely to need tuning, repair, or wholesale change?

Placing Yourself in the Path of Serendipity

66. How often have your plans worked out exactly as intended? How often have your successes happened exactly as planned?
67. Are your current plans premised on success emerging exactly as you anticipate? What if this does not happen?
68. Are you monitoring signs and signals from the marketplace that can both support your expectations, if appropriate, and provide strong evidence when new paths are desirable or necessary?
69. Are your plans formulated in ways that they will support adapting to evolving or new market opportunities, including unexpected opportunities?
70. What mechanisms have you created for making regular reality checks? How well have they worked in the past?

References

Collins, J. C., and Porras, J. I. *Built to Last: Successful Habits of Visionary Companies.* New York: Harper Business, 1994.

Hamel, G. "Strategy as Revolution." *Harvard Business Review,* 1996 (Jul.–Aug.), 69–82.

Kouzes, J. M., and Posner, B. Z. *The Leadership Challenge: How to Get Extraordinary Things Done in Organizations.* San Francisco: Jossey-Bass, 1987.

Leonard-Barton, D. *Wellsprings of Knowledge.* Cambridge: Harvard Business School Press, 1995.

Martin, R. "Changing the Mind of the Corporation." *Harvard Business Review,* 1993 (Nov.–Dec.), 5–12.

Mintzberg, H. "The Manager's Job: Folklore and Fact." *Harvard Business Review,* 1975 (Jul.–Aug.), 49–61.

Peters, T. J., and Waterman, R. H., Jr. *In Search of Excellence: Lessons Learned from America's Best-Run Companies.* New York: Harper & Row, 1982.

Prather, C. W., and Gundry, L. K. *Blueprints for Innovation.* New York: AMACOM, 1996.

Rouse, W. B. *Design for Success: A Human-Centered Approach to Designing Successful Products and Systems.* New York: Wiley, 1991.

Rouse, W. B. *Strategies for Innovation: Creating Successful Products, Systems, and Organizations.* New York: Wiley, 1992.

Rouse, W. B. *Catalysts for Change: Concepts and Principles for Enabling Innovation.* New York: Wiley, 1993.

Rouse, W. B. *Best Laid Plans.* New York: Prentice Hall, 1994.

Rouse, W. B. *Start Where You Are: Matching Your Strategy to Your Marketplace.* San Francisco: Jossey-Bass, 1996.

Senge, P. M. *The Fifth Discipline: The Art and Practice of the Learning Organization.* New York: Doubleday/Currency, 1990.

Simon, H. A. *Models of Man: Social and Rational.* New York: Wiley, 1957.

Taylor, A., III. "Can GM Remodel Itself?" *Fortune,* 1992, *125*(1), 26.

Index